Who Really Killed Claire?

Alan Jackaman

WATERSIDE PRESS

Who Really Killed Claire?

ISBN 978-1-914603-36-5 (Paperback)
ISBN 978-1-914603-37-2 (Epub ebook)
ISBN 978-1-914603-38-9 (Adobe ebook)

A catalogue record for this book can be obtained from the British Library.

Ebook *Who Really Killed Claire?* is available as an ebook including through library models.

Published 2023 by Waterside Press Ltd

WatersidePress.co.uk

Table of Contents

Publisher's Note

The views and opinions expressed in this book are those of the author entirely and honestly held by him. Readers should draw their own conclusions about any claims made or facts and opinions stated, concerning which the possibility of alternative perspectives, narratives, descriptions and interpretations should be borne in mind.

About the Author

Alan Jackaman spent over 25 years as a police officer, including with the first Metropolitan Police dedicated Murder Investigation Team. He later joined its Murder Review Group, examining cold cases/unsolved murders. Commended for his work in bringing serial killer Robert Napper to justice he is the author of *Napper: Through a Glass Darkly* (Waterside Press, 2019), later turned into the Channel 4/Netflix four-part drama *Deceit.*

Acknowledgements

I could not allow this book to be read without acknowledging the help and input of Vincent Wright (who I mention more fully in the *Introduction* and the text). Without his assistance, it would never have been written.

Special thanks are also due to Professor James Grieve and to my long-suffering wife Maria.

Alan Jackaman
March 2023

Acronyms and Abbreviations

ACPO	Association of Chief Police Officers
CPS	Crown Prosecution Service
DC	Detective constable
DCI	Detective chief inspector
D Sgt	Detective sergeant
DI	Detective inspector
D Supt	Detective superintendent
GBH	Grievous bodily harm
HM	His or Her majesty's (as in HM Coroner, HM Prison, etc.)
HOLMES	Home Office Large Major Enquiry System (for computers)
PC	Police constable
PDF	Personal descriptive form
Sgt	Sergeant
SIO	Senior investigating officer
SOCO	Scenes of crime officer
Supt	Superintendent
WPC	Woman police constable.

To the memory of Claire Tiltman and all other victims of mindless, violent crime, especially women and children.

(Claire was just 16 and Jazmine Bisset only four years old).

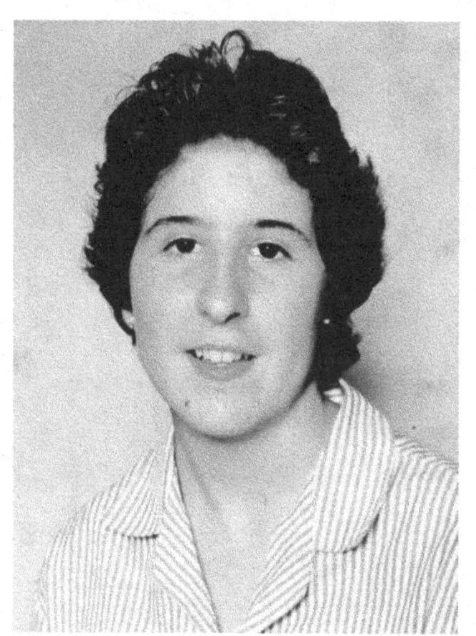

Claire Tiltman.
© PA Photos/Alamy

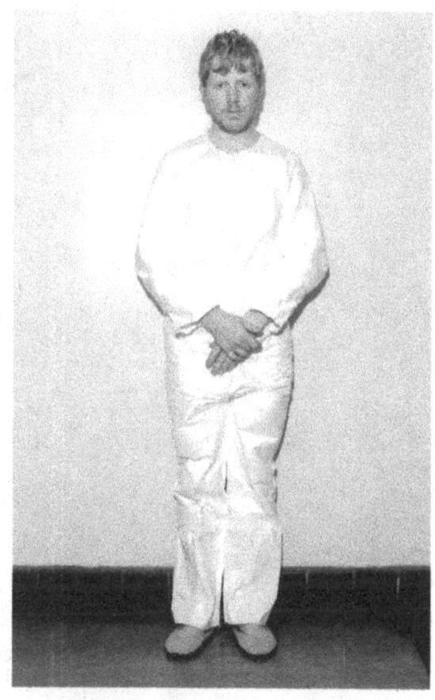

Colin Ash-Smith following arrest in 1995. © Kent Police

Artist's impression of Colin Ash-Smith at his trial in 2014.
© Priscilla Coleman/MB Media

Introduction

'The darkest night will end and the sun will rise.'— Victor Hugo (1802–1885)

But for some this will be an over optimistic viewpoint. In any murder investigation it is important to establish not only the identity of the victim, but their history. This will include their family life, upbringing, schooling, friendships, and a myriad of other tiny details. Details which may or may not prove valuable to the investigator. Most of these nuggets will eventually prove to be irrelevant but occasionally one will become crucial. In the early stages of an enquiry the worth of incoming information cannot sometimes be realised until days, weeks, occasionally years after the event.

It is a well-known fact that most murders are committed within the family circle. This is the first direct path to be viewed. The next line will be friends, which will widen into acquaintances and so on in an ever-expanding circle, which will then include neighbours and those living in the close vicinity. Progress cannot be made until all these avenues are eliminated.

Too many police enquiries, especially those of a high-profile nature, with the attendant media circus, have become bogged down with information coming into the incident room from often far-flung sources. Sometimes wild theorising, and sometimes tinged with malice to feed personal agendas. Although never ignoring any information, the skill of the experienced detective is to distinguish and identify priorities and to investigate from the centre outwards.

No better example of this is the investigation into the Soham murders in Cambridgeshire in August 2002. The local relatively inexperienced murder team were overwhelmed with extraneous information from outlying sources. They somehow overlooked one of the earliest messages put into the system from one of their own sergeants indicating that school caretaker, Ian Huntley, was behaving oddly and required further scrutiny. This message remained languishing in the in-box whilst the investigators fussed over a wave of mostly useless intelligence.

This book reaches into the heart of the investigation of a particularly tragic murder, that of 16-year-old schoolgirl Claire Tiltman. Claire was killed in an apparently motiveless attack in Greenhithe, Kent on 18 January 1993. I wrote the book as a follow up to my previous work, *Napper: Through a Glass Darkly*, which was itself written without any thought of publication but purely as a record of my part in what turned out to be one of the most historically important cases ever to be 'ignored' by a major police force.

Nobody was more surprised than I was when firstly Waterside Press offered to publish that book and subsequently the TV rights were taken up by Channel 4 for their four part drama *Deceit.* I believed that book, once I had finished it, was the end of my writing days and I could at last relax knowing that the truth behind an extraordinary investigation had been aired.

After the publication of *Napper*, I was contacted by many people who had an interest in the case: among them was Vincent Wright who traced me via my publishers. We corresponded first by email, which progressed to telephone calls and eventually a meeting at the Union Jack Club (for ex-service personnel) in Waterloo, London.

Vincent had been struck by some of the revelations in my book about Napper, revelations that despite his own rigorous research were new to him. He was working in his spare time on the Tiltman case and had reached the conclusion that a miscarriage of justice had occurred when Colin Ash-Smith was convicted of Claire's murder and sentenced to life imprisonment. He believed a more likely culprit was Robert Napper, the killer of Samantha and Jazmine Bisset and Rachel Nickell.

At first, I was sceptical. But as Vincent explained the Tiltman case to me, I became more and more involved in the background to Claire's murder. He had, over the years, acquired a vast amount of material, including witness statements, reports of what happened in court, a video of the CPS at work, defence papers and other important records.

There was more than enough for me to conduct a murder review, a practice I had 13 years' experience of whilst working for the Home Office as an investigator of cold cases of this type. In fact, because of Vincent's hard work I had at my disposal more material than from many of the murder reviews I had been tasked with conducting in the past.

Vincent came to me in desperation after being rebuffed by the murder review teams of both the Kent Police and the Metropolitan Police, as well as the Crown Prosecution Service and the judiciary. Virtually everyone he approached seemed determined that the Tiltman case remain closed. This book seeks to remedy that by examining whether Colin Ash-Smith may have been wrongly convicted and that the true killer simply disappeared from the radar of all involved.

Maps

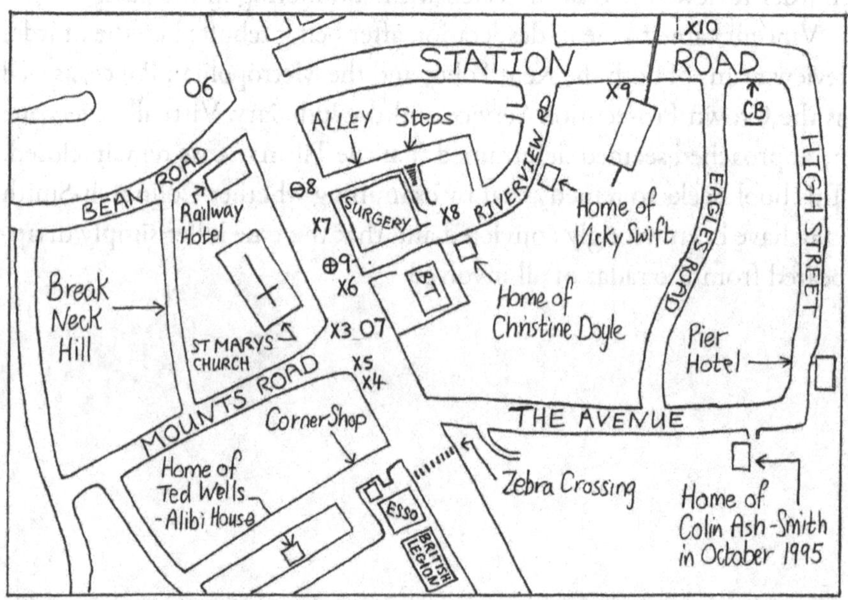

Greenhithe: Central Area as it was in 1993.
Both maps by Vincent Wright.

Legend

O1–O9 Sightings of Claire Tiltman. Symbol O8 has a line through the middle and O9 a cross within it. Respectively these show sightings of Claire as she runs out of the alley (obviously injured). The last one, O9 with the cross, shows where Claire fell and died from her wounds.

X1–X10 Sightings of suspect.

CB Site of attack on Charlotte Barnard, 17 October 1995 (by Colin Ash-Smith).

BG Site of attack on Beverley Godfrey, 21 December 1988 (by Colin Ash-Smith). Approximately ¾ mile south of this mark (i.e. off map).

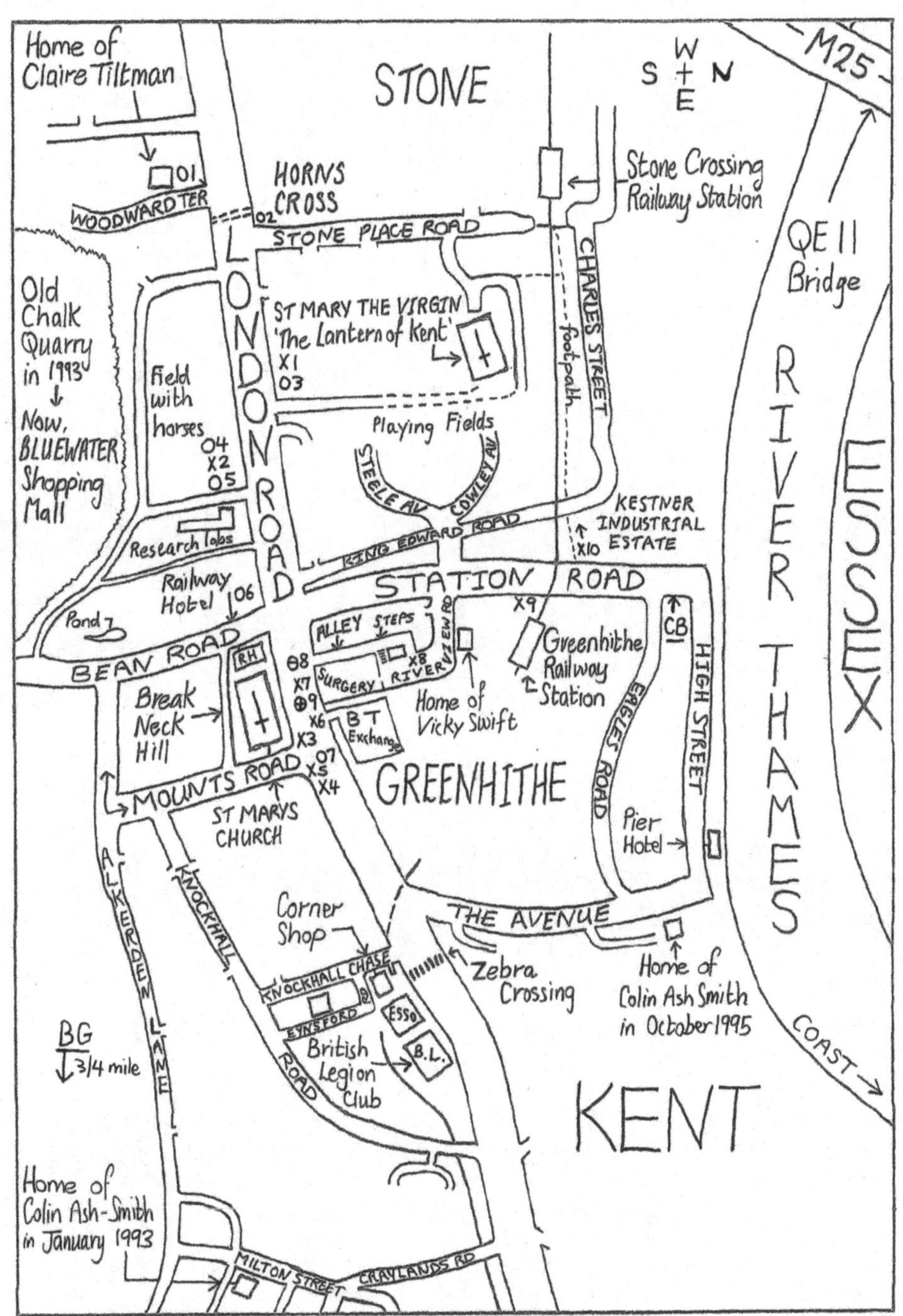

Home of Claire Tiltman
STONE
W S N E
M25
01
WOODWARD TER
HORNS CROSS
02
Stone Crossing Railway Station
STONE PLACE ROAD
CHARLES STREET
footpath
QE II Bridge
Old Chalk Quarry in 1993
Now, BLUEWATER Shopping Mall
LONDON ROAD
ST MARY THE VIRGIN 'The Lantern of Kent'
X1
03
Field with horses
04
X2
05
Playing Fields
STEELE AV
COWLEY AV
RIVER THAMES
ESSEX
KESTNER INDUSTRIAL ESTATE
X10
KING EDWARD ROAD
Research labs
Railway Hotel
06
STATION ROAD
Pond
ALLEY STEPS
X9
Greenhithe Railway Station
CB
BEAN ROAD
RH
X8
RIVER VIEW RD
SURGERY
Home of Vicky Swift
HIGH STREET
Break Neck Hill
X7
X6
X3
BT Exchange
07
X5
X4
EAGLES ROAD
MOUNTS ROAD
GREENHITHE
ST MARYS CHURCH
Pier Hotel
ALKERDEN LANE
KNOCKHALL
Corner Shop
THE AVENUE
KNOCKHALL CHASE
Zebra Crossing
Home of Colin Ash Smith in October 1995
EYNSFORD
ESSO
British Legion Club
B.L.
BG 3/4 mile
ROAD
COAST
KENT
Home of Colin Ash-Smith in January 1993
MILTON STREET
CRAYLANDS RD

Greenhithe: Area Map as it was in 1993.

CHAPTER 1

The Opening

The murder of Claire Tiltman on a dark, windy evening on 18 January 1993 failed to produce a suspect from anywhere within her close family, friends or neighbourly circles. The press had latched onto the case, and it had evolved into, in police parlance, 'a sticker'.

Claire Tiltman was born on 14 January 1977. The only child of Linda (often called Lin) and Cliff Tiltman. She was brought up in a close and loving family in Horns Cross near Greenhithe, a small town in Kent. They lived in quietly residential Woodward Terrace.

Greenhithe is an old port, situated on the southern bank of the Thames Estuary. Originally a fishing village, it developed into an important way station for sailing ships to moor before making their way on the tide up to the Port of London, about 20 miles distant. With the decline of sailing ships and the advent of steam, Greenhithe settled into genteel, gradual, insular, 'irrelevance'. The town began a resurrection in the 1960s with the building of industrial units and new housing, offering a dormitory from London, being only 50 minutes by train from Charing Cross. During Claire's childhood the place retained its village feel. The old sea front escaped 'development' and provided attractive housing plus several well-appointed public houses. From the shoreline the aspect changes to that of an estate of modern housing.

Claire passed her eleven plus exam and attended her local grammar school, where she was a good student and popular with her peers. No information has ever come to light that she was anything other than a bright, typical 16-year-old schoolgirl without an enemy in the world. After finishing school on the Monday evening in question Claire, a young woman of average build with dark curly hair, quite the little tomboy, went straight home and changed from her school uniform into her casual clothes. These comprised a white roll-necked long-sleeved shirt, black trousers and a brown suede leather jacket with a zip up front and elasticated waist and cuffs. She told her mother she was going to meet a friend, Vicky Swift at her house in Riverview Road. Having called out 'Goodbye' to her mother Claire left home a little after 6 pm.

There are witnesses as to exactly where Claire went after leaving home backed up by timings of sightings. These are all dealt with in later chapters but because they are so crucial in identifying or eliminating suspects they are drawn together alongside the distances involved in *Chapter 18.* In that chapter I also seek to demonstrate once and for all that many of the 'so-called facts' concerning time and place alleged in this case do not accord with the known evidence. I have also included a hand drawn map (before this opening chapter) so that readers can better picture the key locations that I need to mention in the book.

As noted, Claire left home a little after 6 pm. She walked by herself down London Road and over the junction (which at the time was a straightforward crossroads) and then up the hill towards Gravesend. There is supposition she may have walked up London Road to a corner shop which is situated in Knockhall Chase, where she may have purchased a packet of ten cigarettes. The shopkeeper could not confirm this, but an opened packet, with one cigarette missing, was found in the jacket pocket on her body.

The corner shop is in the opposite direction to where she had arranged to meet her schoolfriend Vicky Swift in Riverview Road, which is about a mile from Claire's house in Woodward Terrace. If she had visited the shop the natural route to return to her friend Vicky's house would have been back down the hill on London Road. From near the top of the road there is only a footway on one side, the one nearer the river, which would have been on her right side as she walked down the hill. The enquiry seems to have become 'obsessed' with the theory that Claire had walked up the hill to purchase the packet of ten cigarettes.

Near the bottom of the hill on the right-hand side of the road is an entrance to an alleyway that leads to the doctors' surgery in Ivy Bower Close. The alleyway gives a direct route from that part of London Road to Riverview Road and would have been well known to Claire and an obvious choice as a way to her friend in Riverview. In January 1993, the alleyway was usually lit by a streetlamp but at this time it was not working, making the walk between London Road and Riverview on a dark winter's evening an even more threatening experience.

The theory that Claire visited the corner shop at the top of London Road and was walking back down the hill becomes far less plausible in the light of what I later say in this book (see especially *Chapter 18* where the times involved are set out in detail). There is no doubt she was in London Road very near to the alley entrance. The cut through it provided would be an obvious shortcut to her friend's house in Riverview Road. The alternative route would have entailed a much longer walk, down to the London Road junction and a circular tour back towards Riverview Road (see the map).

Claire either turned into or was forced into the alleyway and, once there, was stabbed repeatedly. Her wounds were not survivable, and she quickly collapsed to the ground where she soon died. The attack was not witnessed and her assailant did not remain at the scene. It isn't known which way this person fled except that it was highly unlikely it was in the same direction as Claire who was seen to emerge from the alleyway alone and collapse on the pavement of London Road next to the alleyway's exit.

These are the bare facts which prompted one of the largest ever murder enquiries in the county of Kent.

View down the alley towards London Road. The steps lead to the doctor's surgery, Ivy Bower Close and Riverview Road, where the victim's friend Vicky Swift lived. © Vincent Wright

Tiny memorial garden and plaque to Claire Tiltman and D Supt Owen Taylor. This is where Claire died, about five yards outside the alley on London Road. © Vincent Wright

Stone Crossing Railway Station. © Vincent Wright

CHAPTER 2

The Crime Scene

Michael Godfrey left work in Northfleet and drove his Jaguar XJS along the B255 towards Greenhithe. With him was a work colleague, Ron Wilson. By the time they reached the junction with the A226 Gravesend road it was dark and Godfrey had his headlights on. The roads were dry and visibility good as he waited at the traffic lights before turning right into London Road. The lights changed to green, and he turned up the hill towards Gravesend. Just after the junction he noticed on the near side, lying on the pavement, what appeared to him to be a black bundle. As he passed, he saw a flash of white on it and immediately declared to Ron his passenger, 'It's a person.' Ron replied, 'No, it's a bag of rubbish.'

Undeterred Godfrey stopped the car and reversed back close to where the bundle lay. He put his hazard warning lights on, got out of the car, and walked over. His suspicions were quickly confirmed as he came up to what he initially thought was a young male. The 'person' was on their knees with their coat rucked up their back over a white blouse, gasping for breath. Godfrey who had some knowledge of first aid knelt beside the person and saw large pooling of blood through the blouse. He realised now that it was a young female. It was in fact Claire Tiltman.

Godfrey laid Claire on her back with her head pointing up the hill. He spoke to her, giving words of reassurance but she gave no response. He tried mouth to mouth resuscitation but found her airways blocked with blood. He then attempted heart compression and feeling no pulse he realised Claire had died in his arms. He directed Ron Wilson to go over the road to the Railway Hotel[1] to call for an ambulance while he stayed with Claire until it arrived.

Wilson was able to be more specific about the time; he estimated they turned into the junction at 6.20 pm. He left Godfrey to administer first aid and ran to the Railway Hotel where he asked someone to call for an ambulance. That telephone call was made by customer Christine Bance and registered as having been received at 6.23 pm. Wilson then made his way back to Claire to see the first ambulance arrive only two minutes later, quickly followed by the police. Michael Godfrey and Ron Wilson both remained at the scene assisting the police and ambulance crews. At some stage, a police officer asked Wilson to move Godfrey's Jaguar further up the road which he did. They stayed at the scene until 8.20 pm before going over to the Railway Hotel to clean up and go home.

At 6.20 pm PC 5471 Nicholas Allen was driving his marked police car on an emergency call along the main road from Bean in the direction of Greenhithe. With him was WPC 9139 Ann Martin.[2] As PC Allen approached the junction with London Road he slowed as the lights were against him. As he traversed the junction, he saw two ambulances parked back-to-back in London Road opposite St Mary's Church. He continued on his original call until at 6.28 pm he received another radio message redirecting him to London Road to deal with a 'serious road traffic accident'.

Within two minutes he arrived back at the point where he had seen the two ambulances. WPC Martin was the first one out of the police car and went to where Claire lay; she was immediately informed by one of the ambulance crew, 'This is no accident. She has been stabbed.' PC Allen overheard this and immediately started cordoning off the area, whilst WPC Martin started to take the details of the people who were present at the scene. PC Allen radioed in for further assistance and to notify the CID.

At 6.48 pm, PC Allen was informed by the medical team that they were unable to resuscitate Claire. He directed WPC Martin to go to the

1. These premises have been known as the Railway Hotel, Railway Tavern, Railway Tavern Hotel or, historically, by other names. No longer a hotel or public house they house a fast food outlet.
2. Her statements refer to PC Ann Martin but I have used WPC for clarity.

far end of the alleyway and prevent any pedestrians walking towards and subsequently over the scene. He was very soon joined by DC Hancock and PC Connor from the local CID who took over management of the crime scene. Those such as the one where Claire was murdered are inherently difficult to manage. It was in a public place where the public had open access. It was at a time when footfall was at its peak from commuters returning from the railway station to their homes. It was open to the elements and the elements were not being kind, very windy and rain was threatened at any moment, this coupled with the fact that being mid-January it was already dark.

There is always an unavoidable chaotic opening to a crime scene where the first and overriding objective is the preservation of life. Naturally, members of the public and the medics involved have little thought in the heat of the moment for the preservation of evidence. That duty falls to the police and the first officers to arrive at the scene made a creditable start. They were there within minutes and almost immediately set up a cordon and started to collect the identities of those present. Back up assistance was speedily sent for and a representative of the CID, DC Hancock was quickly at the scene followed by DI Turner who, realising he had a murder on his hands, informed D Supt Owen Taylor who arrived to take control and establish a murder enquiry team. All detectives receive training in the preservation of crime scenes and should be well-versed in the handling of potential exhibits.

The police surgeon Dr Shanks was summoned at 6.51 pm. He was at his home and immediately left to attend. The role of the police surgeon at these events is not, as some may imagine from various exaggerated TV dramas, to solve the crime. Their main function is to pronounce death and establish a continuity point for the subsequent post mortem. Dr Shanks introduced himself to DI Turner at 7.19 pm and made an assessment. He noted three stab wounds in the chest area which were visible without disturbing or moving the body. He made a judgement that on the evidence of the large pooling of blood, death was not instantaneous, and Claire had bled for some time before expiring. Whilst making his examination Dr Shanks touched a packet of cigarettes which were in Claire's jacket pocket. He made a note of this. He pronounced Claire dead and left the scene.

Scenes of crime officer (SOCO) Mercer was contacted at 7.30 pm and arrived at 8 pm. By this time the press was buzzing with enquiries and a dedicated press line was set up at the police switchboard. SOCO Mercer made a photographic record of the scene and then concentrated on picking up medical debris from the area which was starting to blow around in the stiffening wind. These items he placed in exhibits bags before concentrating in more detail on the scene itself. In the gutter of London Road just nine feet from Claire's feet he found a broken gold earring with red flecks on it. He placed this in an exhibit bag and marked it Exhibit CJM/3. In the alleyway he found another piece of the earring, a clasp, this he labelled Exhibit CJM/4. The earring was later identified as Claire's and would seem to indicate she was attacked first in the alleyway and the struggle continued back towards its entrance with London Road.

At this stage the identity of the victim was still unknown. At 8.50 pm Mrs Linda Tiltman contacted Dartford Police Station to report her daughter Claire was overdue returning home. She told them that Claire had left home wearing black trousers, a white polo neck top and a brown suede leather jacket, saying she was 5' 4" tall with dark hair and a fair complexion.

Linda Tiltman, with a feeling of dread, made her way to Vicky Swift's house, Claire's friend in Riverview Road. It was here that police found her and requested she return home. Police from the murder team then called at her home address and gave her the tragic news of Claire's murder. Claire's father, Cliff, was collected from his place of work in London at around 11 pm to prepare him to identify the body of his daughter at the mortuary at West Hill Hospital, Dartford.

At 10.37 pm, the on-call Home Office accredited pathologist, Dr Michael Heath, arrived. He was shown the victim's body, which, was lying in the same position on its back, on the pavement of London Road, next to the alleyway. His attention was immediately drawn to the cut clothing on her chest and jacket sleeves. He correctly assumed this had been done by the ambulance crew. He was also drawn to the extensive blood staining over her white polo neck shirt and her brassiere and nearby on the adjacent wall and pavement.

SOCO Mercer then assisted him to prepare Claire's body for transfer to the mortuary where at 11.45 pm Dr Heath carried out a post mortem. Also present during this examination were D Supt Taylor, D I Turner, DC McManus, exhibits officer, Charles Wright, principal SOCO, Robert Green, senior SOCO, HM Coroner's Officer Janice Goldfarb, and Keith Challinger, senior anatomical mortuary technician. Quite a crowd.

Before them was the well-nourished body of a young female, 156 cm in height weighing 55 kilograms. She was wearing a suede jacket unzipped at the front, a white roll-necked long-sleeved shirt, a brassiere in place but with a cut on the right strap and stab like cuts through both brassiere cups. Her black ski pants were held by a belt pulled into the last hole. She wore black tights with extensive laddering on the right thigh, white pants and heavy lace up black boots which were in the lace up mode. It is pertinent to note that the roll-neck shirt was tucked into the ski pants and over the tights. This would obviously negate any penetrative sexual assault on the lower part of her body. She wore a watch on her left wrist and four bangles on her right wrist. A necklace was intact around her neck.

Both ears were pierced and there was a loop earring in the right ear without the butterfly attachment. This would be found to correspond with the broken earring found earlier by SOCO Mercer at the murder scene. There were four holes over the back of her jacket and a slice to the top of the left side next to the zip near the neckline. There were six puncture holes in the right-hand side front of her roll-neck shirt.

Dr Heath recorded a small bruise over the centre of the upper lip and the right side of the lower lip. Claire had been stabbed nine times. Many of which individually would have proved fatal. All wounds, bar one, were to the right side of her body, two in her back and seven to her front. The weapon (which wasn't recovered) had a blade approximately 2.8 cm wide and between 13 and 15 cm long. It was single edged.

Dr Heath deduced the most likely first wound was to her left breast. In his opinion the following five blows were consistent with the assailant standing to the *right* of the victim and with her jacket being pulled away to one side. Two stab wounds were consistent with the assailant standing behind the victim. Dr Heath rightly qualified his findings by stating that no conclusions could be drawn until the wounds were compared to the murder weapon. Later in his report he mentioned a 5 cm by 1.5 cm bruise on the outer left thigh which was consistent with having been caused by a 'firm' blow. There was no sign of sexual interference or sexual assault and there were no defensive wounds. A second post mortem was later carried out by Dr Peter Jerreat. This is completely normal procedure where there is no suspect as the defence is entitled to its own autopsy. Without a suspect this second autopsy is carried out in the defence's absence.

SOCO Mercer remained at the crime scene collating evidence after Claire's body was removed. He made another detailed examination of the scene, a task performed in ever-deteriorating weather conditions. He took and preserved blood samples from the alleyway and from London Road. He assessed from the 'area of stagger' that Claire had been initially attacked in the alleyway and staggered back to the low wall at the alleyway entrance at the junction with London Road where she was found by Michael Godfrey. Examination of the scene in the middle of the night was now exhausted and had been taken as far as it could go in the circumstances.

CHAPTER 3

Any Suspects?

The incident room was set up in Dartford Police Station under the command of D Supt Owen Taylor and an operational name assigned to the enquiry, codenamed Operation Artist. The day after the murder, Taylor, after a long night, gave his initial briefing to his team. The scene had already been revisited in daylight and no obvious further leads could be found to give any indication as to who was responsible. The enquiry had been given a Home Office Large Major Enquiry System (HOLMES) account specifically designed to cope with large enquiries. Lines of enquiry were set up which included expanding the house-to-house enquiries which had been started the night before and also research into local sex offenders.

The onerous task of informing Claire's parents of her brutal death had been done. It was news they would never recover from. It is difficult to imagine losing any child, but to lose an only, adored child in such hideous circumstances goes beyond any understanding. The victim was a complete innocent. She'd had no involvement in any criminal activity, had no known romantic involvement and was universally well-liked. There was no apparent sexual motive to the attack. Taylor had a real problem on his hands. The only option left to him was the grindingly slow and painful work of setting up the incident room and collating all information, however off-kilter that information might be and exploring every avenue thoroughly.

Witnesses were starting to come forward with various sightings of a male seen behind Claire, in London Road, just prior to the attack and just after in Riverview Road. Another witness, Danny French, saw a male walking in front of Claire. The suspicious sightings and their timings are dealt with in greater detail later (see particularly *Chapter 18*). A list of local possible suspects was made. At the top of the list was a young man who had attended the scene after the ambulance crew had arrived.

Peter Brookes was a local man aged 19. He had appeared at the alleyway minutes after Michael Godfrey, Ron Wilson and the medics. He hovered in the background showing a keen interest and questioning police and others present as to what had happened. He remained at the scene long after the police arrived and further drew attention to himself by continuously interfering with fatuous enquiries until he was eventually asked to leave after giving his details to police. After leaving the scene Brookes telephoned his father from a public call box and told him he had come across a girl who had been stabbed and that first aid hadn't worked, and she'd died. He was, not unnaturally, upset.

After this telephone call Brookes called in on a young woman who lived in a flat above the one where he lived and told her, 'A bloke is running around stabbing people.' He embellished the picture by telling her he had found Claire slumped against a fence bleeding profusely but that he was unable to close the wound. The neighbour noticed blood on Brookes' fingernails. Brookes then informed her that the police would be coming to 'pick him up' shortly. He then returned to the scene, arriving just before midnight and further questioned another police officer about what had happened.

Eventually Brookes returned to his flat. The following morning, he again went to the scene, where, to his joy, he found the press and television crews gathered. Wasting no time, he informed the media teams of his part in the incident. He was filmed by TV cameras as he gave his exaggerated account of his part in events. That same evening WPC Ann Martin, one of the two officers first on the scene, saw Brookes on TV and recognised him as the man who had been behaving oddly near the area of the murder. The next day, Wednesday January 20, he was picked up by a *Daily Mail* reporter at around 11 am in London Road and taken to outside Dartford Police Station where members of the press were gathered ready to interview him. He gave another press conference after which he walked into the police station to provide an official account to officers.

By now Brookes was starting to believe his own story. He told the police he had found Claire slumped by a wall and was shortly afterwards joined by two other men. He saw the stab wounds which, in his opinion, were inflicted by a four-inch lock-knife. The police let Brookes finish his story whilst becoming ever more suspicious of him as it did not coincide with what was known about his behaviour at the scene. He appeared to be giving information about the stab wounds which only the assailant would have known.

On the afternoon of Wednesday January 20, Brookes was arrested at Dartford Police Station on suspicion of murdering Claire. His flat was searched, and he was interviewed over two days. At first Brookes maintained his statement was accurate, but by the time of his sixth and final interview his story changed to one more approximating to his minimal involvement. He admitted telling the police 'a load of cobblers'. This, according to Brookes, was as a result of his being misquoted by the press. Brookes also accounted for the blood under his nails as a result of an earlier nosebleed.

Police expended a great deal of time and energy in verifying Brookes' final version of events. Scrapings from his nails were submitted along with a Bowie knife seized in his flat and his leather jacket. All these items were forensically examined and showed no trace from the scene. Quite apart from the arrest and interviews, 67 police actions were raised as a result, and 54 statements were taken from individuals pertaining directly to Brookes. Fourteen messages and 40 documents were also raised. This incident brings into focus how, on this type of enquiry, a Walter Mitty-type character, seemingly trying to enhance his lowly stature can result in a lot of time being wasted by police. Brookes was eliminated from the enquiry.

Throughout the investigation into the murder, 47 individuals reached the qualifying level of 'suspect'. The majority were eliminated quickly; others (as in the case of Brookes) required a far more thorough examination. As the enquiry progressed and faltered the enquiry team had to widen their net. Without any firm forensic evidence from the scene of the murder, not a single witness and no apparent motive they were on an uphill struggle.

On 10 March 1993, two months after Claire's death, Brian Atkins attended Stone House Hospital Dartford in a highly emotional state. He shouted at the nursing staff and threatened to commit suicide with some tablets he was holding. The staff were unable to calm him before he ran off returning shortly afterwards with a knife with which he threatened the staff. This time he was eventually pacified and was sectioned under the Mental Health Act, which meant he was kept in a secure ward for his own and others' safety. Four days later Atkins made an emergency 999 call from Joyce Green Hospital telling the operator he was being held against his will and, furthermore, that he wished to confess to the murder of Claire Tiltman.

On hearing the news of Atkin's confession, the investigating team felt a surge of relief as, almost two months into the enquiry, they still did not have a firm suspect. When later interviewed by police, Atkins denied Claire's murder and said he had no memory of what he was doing on the date of her death. No statement was taken from Atkins because of his fragile mental state but all subsequent enquiries could not link him to the killing. Atkins was eliminated as a credible suspect.

John Cotter entered the enquiry when he told police he had seen a male who he didn't know sitting on the low wall by the church path opposite the murder scene. Cotter claimed to have seen this person in the same place at the same time, 2 pm, over a period of four days from the 13 to 16 January 1993. Cotter had seen an e-fit provided by Lee Delguidice a 12-year-old boy who saw a suspect moving away from the scene after the murder towards Stone Crossing Railway Station. The sighting by Delguidice is interesting in itself as it refers to a man he saw near the scene at the relevant time. This and other sightings of other unidentified possible suspects will be looked at in detail. Police believed the e-fit resembled Cotter. Accordingly, Cotter was invited to the police station where he gave his account in a tape-recorded interview. He was asked directly if he had murdered Claire which he denied. There was nothing else to link him to the enquiry.

As already indicated the list of possible suspects grew over the years to 47. The deputy senior investigating officer (SIO) DI Withers included various types of what might be described as 'the usual suspects.' Others on the list were obviously suffering from varying degrees of mental illness or had been offered up with little substantive evidence and were clearly prompted through grudges or fantasy.

The firmest suspect on the list was a man called Peter Rivers. Rivers drew attention to himself in the most dramatic of ways. A man suffering severe mental health problems he lived locally with his mother. Rivers had stabbed his mother to death in February 1994 and then committed suicide, but not before writing out a scrawled suicide note in which he stated he had killed his mother because she had suspected him of killing Claire. Police thoroughly investigated Rivers to establish if there were any links between him and Claire Tiltman. He featured as a possible suspect, but nothing was ever found to link him to Claire or her murder.

One interesting character included on the suspect list was 'No. 32: Robert Clive Napper'. It is worth reproducing in full the entry made against his name by the deputy SIO. It can be seen to have been made years after the murder of Claire as it refers to the conviction of Napper for the murder of Rachel Nickell and the trial for that offence was not until December 2008, 15 years after Claire Tiltman was killed. In the words of the then deputy SIO:

> 'Napper came into the investigation as a result of his conviction for the killing of Rachel Nickel [sic] on Wimbledon Common and Samantha and Jazmine Bisset in London.
>
> He is currently detained at Broadmoor Hospital for those crimes.
>
> There are no connections identified between the murder of Claire Tiltman and the murders committed by Napper. Rachel Nickel [sic] was murdered on Wimbledon in daylight hours in company with her son, the Bisset murders took place in their own home. Rachel Nickel [sic] and Samantha Bisset were both subject of sexual assaults. Claire Tiltman was murdered in an alley next to a busy road in the hours of darkness. Napper frequented the London area and not Kent. There is no evidence to connect Napper to the Claire Tiltman murder.'

The rather brusque, dismissively short report above ignores several important factors. The Nickell murder, as stated, was on open land during the hours of daylight, the Bisset murders in a private dwelling, during the hours of darkness. Neither, on its own, bears any comparison with the murder of Claire. However, it is pertinent to note that they do not bear any obvious similarities to each other either. This underlines how random Napper was in his choice of victim. Also not mentioned, but which should have been taken into account, is the series of rapes committed by Napper, mostly in 1992 and of progressively increasing violence. These are known as 'The Green Chain Rapes' and were carried out on common land and footpaths not hidden from any chance discovery by any member of the public (see further *Chapters 4* and *8*).

Although it may be assumed both Rachel and Samantha were victims of sexual violence, the exact nature and application of the sexual motivation is unknown. No semen was found at either crime scene and no evidence of penetration by sexual congress. It would seem that, although sex was the prime motivator, the assailant was either incapable of, or disinclined to commit the act of sexual intercourse. If there was no overt 'sexual' motive in the murder of Claire, what then *was* the motive?

The flat statement that 'Napper frequented the London area and not Kent' is just not true. Napper was born and raised in Abbey Wood which, although it is within the administrative boundary of the London Borough of Bexley, is still geographically within the county of Kent. It is a short, direct, four stop train journey from Plumstead (where Napper was living in 1993) to Greenhithe. Napper, not being a driver, relied totally on bus and rail networks of which he had an encyclopaedic knowledge.

Operation Artist (the investigation into the murder of Claire Tiltman) seems to have fallen into a similar 'quagmire trap' that the murder team in Wimbledon fell into concerning Rachel Nickell. Napper was dismissed as a suspect because all of his crimes were in south east London and the Bisset's were murdered in their home. Wimbledon is in the far west of London, miles from Eltham where Napper lived when he killed Rachel. After her murder he moved to Plumstead to avoid giving a blood sample. Plumstead is within easy reach of Greenhithe, and much closer than it is to Wimbledon which is a tortuous journey from south east London but which, nevertheless, we now know was one made by Napper to kill Rachel Nickell. With every new piece of knowledge we achieve greater understanding of what happened.

CHAPTER 4

An Insider's View

It is at this juncture I give an insider's view and declare my interest in Robert Napper. I was the arresting officer of Napper for the murder of Samantha and Jazmine Bisset who were killed in their flat at Heathfield Terrace, Plumstead on 3 November 1993. That particularly notorious case, which involved not only the killing of Samantha and her evisceration, but most shockingly the sexual assault and murder of her four-year-old daughter Jazmine, did not arouse any great interest from the media. Consequently it caused barely a ripple to the powers at New Scotland Yard. It was viewed as of little importance in the great scheme of things. Time and hindsight would reveal just what a massive misjudgement this was.

Everyone with any interest in these matters will have little trouble remembering the murder of Rachel Nickell on Wimbledon Common on 15 July 1992. The names of Samantha and Jazmine are not so well known and remained in obscurity until Napper's belated conviction for Rachel's murder. Subsequent to Napper's conviction for the murder of Rachel the names of Samantha and Jazmine Bisset have reached a considerably higher profile. In hindsight the patterns linking the crimes seem glaringly obvious but, at the time, any connection between the two cases was dismissed out of hand by the Nickell enquiry team.

The factors at the time seemed to add up to absolutely no similarities between the two cases. Without any leads it was a natural progression to rule out a connection between the two. Rachel was killed during daylight, on a sunny day in a public place, whilst she was with her two-year-old child Alex, who was left unharmed. Samantha and Jazmine were killed in their home by someone who had broken in during the hours of darkness.

A psychological profiler, Paul Britton (now Professor Britton) who had been called in to consider both cases deemed that it was likely that the Nickell killer would be living close to the area where she was murdered. Finally and far more significantly, the Nickell team had a strong suspect in the guise of Colin Stagg, who ticked all of their profile boxes and also, as stated in Britton's profile, lived within easy walking distance of Wimbledon Common (and regularly walked his dog Brandy there).

Colin Stagg was already in the Wimbledon team's sights long before the murder of Samantha and Jazmine in Plumstead in November 1993. The investigation into the Plumstead murder had hit its own problems with the Bisset murder team having no obvious suspect. Napper wasn't identified as a suspect until six months had passed and wasn't arrested until May 1994. By this time Colin Stagg had been charged on the 13 August 1993 with the Nickell murder and been remanded in custody until his trial on 14 September 1994. At least being in custody gave Stagg the perfect alibi for the Bisset murders.

Subsequent to the arrest of Napper in Plumstead in May 1994 he was quickly linked to a series of rapes which preceded the Bisset murders. All of these rape attacks were on ground open to the public. They were all in south east London along a series of footpaths which are collectively known as the Green Chain Walk. This stretches from Lewisham through woods and parks down to Eltham and on to the River Thames at Thamesmead.

The SIOs on Operation Eccleston, the Green Chain Rapes enquiry, closed down the investigation into the rape series after the attacks seemed to stop following the rape of a young mother in the presence of her two-year-old child on 24 May 1992 in King John's Walk, Eltham. This last known victim had walked the tranquil footpath from Eltham towards Mottingham before she noticed a male figure in the distance. When she next looked up, the figure had disappeared from her view. As she passed the point where she had last seen the man, a figure appeared behind her. She heard footsteps rapidly gaining on her and before she had time to react a ligature had been thrown over her neck and tightened. She instinctively let go of her child's buggy and grabbed the cord.

A rough voice told her to put her hands behind her back and, as she did so, the ligature was loosened. She pleaded for the sake of her little girl and was told to 'shut up.' After several blows to her face and body she was flung to the ground where an attempt was made to rape her. This failed, as the assailant could not achieve an erection. Without warning the attacker suddenly stood up, pulled up his Y-front-style underpants and shorts and ran off in the direction of Eltham. There was never any suggestion that the attacker was in possession of a knife but the injuries to the victim were severe. She suffered heavy bruising to her head and upper body. Her right eye was so badly damaged she had loss of vision and required laser treatment to correct it. Her description of the attacker was understandably hazy, but she said he was aged between 26 and 30 years, slim with short brown hair, dirty grey teeth and a spotty chin.

Her description, given to the first police officer to attend, differed from her eventual statement. The reporting officer was unusually tall, even for a police officer, and when establishing the suspect's height asked, 'I'm 6' 3", was he as tall as me?' An excellent way to judge height and with more chance of accuracy than the arbitrary question 'How tall was he?' She replied, 'About your height.' This description of a taller attacker was inexplicably amended in her later written statement to read 5' 7", thus placing him well within the height parameters of the suggested suspect of the previous assaults of between 5' 6" and 5' 10".

From the victim a specimen of DNA established the attacker to be the same man who had attacked at least three other women on the Green Chain Walk within the previous three months, the first on 10 March 1992. There were probably many more attacks, but the DNA evidence from the four attacks showed the attacker to have been the same person. Unfortunately, the DNA was not recorded on the criminal index without which the police could only wait until they had a suspect to match their DNA sample.

At the time of the sexual assault in King John's Walk, Eltham on 24 May 1992, Napper was living in Eltham, in Well Hall Road. He was identified to police from two separate sources who stated that he bore a resemblance to the circulated Photofit. Both of these witnesses followed up by saying they knew Napper (one from work, one a neighbour) and both expanded on their information detailing his strange behaviour. Detectives were duly dispatched to see Napper in August 1992. They found him at his then address at Well Hall Road where he lodged in a single room. They found him to be co-operative, quiet and unflustered. They also found him to be 6' 1" tall. Not deterred, they requested Napper to attend Eltham Police Station to give a sample to be tested against the DNA profile. This came one month after the Nickell murder which had been in July and three months after the last known rape offence on the Green Chain Walk in May. The neighbour also informed police that he had heard from Napper's fellow lodgers that he had had his bags packed for weeks.

Napper failed to show up for his DNA sample on September 2. He was then informed that the appointment was now rescheduled for September 8, a date which Napper also failed to keep. Quite apart from the obvious suspicions which would have been raised by any person failing to give a sample after two requests, the timing of offences is also worthy of closer inspection.

The first request was only three months after the last rape and only one month after the murder of Rachel Nickell, although it must be remembered that the Green Chain Rapes enquiry team had no inkling that the Green Chain Rapist was also responsible for the Wimbledon murder. By the time of the second request in September 1992 the rape enquiry was in full shut down mode and the fateful decision was made by the SIO to eliminate Napper as he wasn't within the height parameters and not pursue the demand for a DNA sample.

The series of Green Chain Rapes happened predominantly in the first half of 1992. Rachel Nickell was murdered in Wimbledon in July 1992. On the face of things there was absolutely nothing to link these offences with the murder in Greenhithe of Claire Tiltman in January 1993. In any event by the time of Claire's murder the Wimbledon operation had identified a suspect for their murder. Indeed, they really only had the one, that man was Colin Stagg. They became almost completely focused on Stagg.

The murder of Samantha and Jazmine Bisset in November 1993 did not throw up any obvious suspect initially either. An approach was made to the Wimbledon investigation to sound out the possibility it may have been committed by the same hand. This hypothesis was dismissed by the Wimbledon investigation. They had a firm suspect in Colin Stagg and, at the time of the Bisset murders, Stagg was shut up in prison awaiting trial for the Nickell murder. A faultless alibi. The obverse, that the Bisset killer may have also murdered Rachel Nickell and Stagg was innocent, was not considered. It was such a radical supposition, and it flew in the face of all their work in constructing a case against Stagg.

the Wimbledon investigation to sound out the possibility it may have been committed by the same person. This hypothesis was dismissed by the Wimbledon investigation. They had a firm suspect in Colin Stagg and at the time of the Bisset murders, Stagg was already in prison awaiting trial for the Nickell murder. A [illegible] stall [illegible]. That [illegible] that the Bisset killer may have also murdered Rachel Nickell so [illegible] was innocent, was not considered. It was such a radical supposition and [illegible] the [illegible] of all [illegible] case against Stagg.

CHAPTER 5

Forensics

The scene at the alleyway in London Road, Greenhithe did not lend itself to the collection of pristine evidence. It was an area frequented by the general public and night had fallen before the investigation had a chance to get under way. The victim when found was in a critical condition and consequently was surrounded by members of the medical profession intent on the overriding concern of saving her life.

A number of footprints were found at or near the scene. Many of these were later identified as belonging to ambulance crews and other people who had lawful access. The shoeprints which were recovered were carefully collated and preserved for elimination and for comparison with the footwear of any suspect who may have later entered the frame. At this early stage of the enquiry, no firm suspect was remotely in the picture.

Samples of blood were taken from all areas in the vicinity of where Claire was found. Because of the blood pooling and patterning, it became clear that she had been attacked in the alleyway and staggered back to London Road where she collapsed by the low wall near the entrance to the alleyway. All of the blood samples collected, with the exception of the arterial spray on the fence, were on later analysis shown to come from Claire. There is always an outside possibility that in such a frenzied attack the perpetrator might injure themself and leave their own blood at the scene. This did not appear to be the case here. The blood on the wooden fence had been contaminated by preservative and exposure to the elements. The only conclusion that could be reached was that it was human blood. However, given the circumstances, it is extremely likely the blood came from Claire.

In all cases of this seriousness, it is imperative to seize and preserve as much as possible from the crime scene, however obscure this may seem. The object is to tie in any future suspect. If the suspect is yet to be identified this becomes even more crucial, as the exhibits may be needed months or even years down the line. The highest regard and care must be given to the preservation of the clothing of the victim. In 1993 the use of DNA in criminal investigations was still in its infancy. It is now taken for granted to be a tool in the investigators' armoury but, in the early 1990s, the very concept of allowing DNA evidence in a criminal trial was still open to challenge.

Also, we must bear in mind that the science of DNA has now reached a sophistication undreamt of in the early 1990s. To obtain a DNA profile scientists would have needed a blood sample the size of a five-penny piece before having a good chance of extracting that profile. The days of obtaining DNA profiles from cigarette butts or items merely touched, involving enhanced short tandem repeat (STR) methods were still far into the future.

It is the rare investigator who takes into account the possibilities of utilising improvements which may happen in the future by preserving exhibits accordingly. The clothing Claire wore at the time, more specifically her jacket and roll (or polo) neck blouse, were subjected to intense testing. Some of these tests did not take into account the development of DNA and, logically, why would they? Investigators need to go on what they have and are not clairvoyants. Although carried out with the best of intentions the handling and testing of Claire's jacket may have destroyed any chance of enhanced DNA testing. For instance, 'control stabbings' were undertaken on the material to compare the knife cuts. There can be no criticism of these tests and the fact that they were done should not in any case rule out further testing.

As recorded in the Rachel Nickell enquiry, the original DNA tests carried out on Rachel's clothes showed a negative result. In the Nickell case it wasn't until 13 years later, when the clothes were re-submitted for further analysis, that a profile was discovered of alien DNA. This DNA sample did not, as is supposed, point to a particular suspect but what it did do was to eliminate every other suspect in the enquiry, narrowing the suspect field to one individual. Further advances in DNA allowed the sample to be further refined and a positive DNA cross-reference was made, matching without any doubt to the last remaining suspect, Robert Clive Napper.

It should also be borne in mind that it is known Napper hardly, if ever, wore gloves during any of his attacks, even at the murders of Samantha and Jazmine inside their flat. An attack which he had planned meticulously. In Napper's curious logic the idea of fingerprints did not enter the equation. And they so nearly didn't when his fingerprints were confused with those of Samantha Bisset, slowing the investigation down by six months.

When no obvious suspect came to light for the Tiltman attack, the investigators then spent a great deal of time and effort on identifying whose shoeprints belonged to whom. Because the scene had originally been classified as a road traffic accident and there was a chance of saving Claire's life the immediate scene was heavily disturbed with many shoe marks. Nevertheless, the majority of these were matched. They were attributed to ambulance and police personnel. These shoe marks near to where Claire collapsed would likely have obliterated any marks left by the suspect. The investigators, realising this, cast their net wider and incorporated the entire alleyway and the entrance to the doctors' surgery at the end of Ivy Bower Close, where three paving slabs were removed as possible evidence.

It is unclear from the available documents where exactly the outstanding shoeprints are from. All known visitors to the area had their footwear compared to Exhibits CJM/1A, CJM/1B and CJM/1C. Two of the three prints, presumably photographed by SOCO Chris Mercer, CJM/1A and 1B were Dr Marten boot-type prints (as worn by ambulance staff) and found very close to Claire. The third however, CJM/1C was found in the alleyway and appeared to be a shoeprint. It was checked against all witnesses known to have been at the scene and also those who had come forward as a result of an appeal locally for any other person who had used the alleyway before the incident.

Two BT engineers came forward, Kevin French and Stephen Edgely. They disclosed they had used the alleyway on their way to work in the nearby BT compound. Both were wearing shoes of the Reebok brand; neither matched the outstanding shoeprint.

Vincent Wright (mentioned in my Introduction) requested from Kent Police via the Freedom of Information Act all relevant information regarding Exhibit CJM/1C. But this request was turned down. Vincent tried again during a meeting with Kent detectives at Northfleet Police Station in 2020. His request was again refused. CJM/1C does exist, or more worryingly, has existed, but its whereabouts and the shoe patterning it offers are unknown to the public. It would be very interesting to compare trainer print CJM/1C to the trainer shoeprint left at the scene of the Bisset murder in Heathfield Terrace, Plumstead by Napper in November 1993.

Napper also left shoe marks at the Nickell scene. A suspect was seen to be apparently washing his hands in a nearby culvert. An impression of a shoeprint taken from where he was seen remained on file in the Nickell case. It was not until the case was reviewed many years later that the worth of that shoeprint was realised. When Napper was arrested in 1994, he wore a pair of working shoes. These were seized on his arrival at Bexleyheath Police Station. The Bisset murder team had little interest in these shoes at the time because their suspect was known to have committed the murders of the Bissets whilst wearing Adidas trainers.

After Napper's trial and conviction for the Bisset murders most of his personal property was returned to him. Amongst those items were the working shoes worn during his arrest. They followed him to Broadmoor High Security Hospital where they were put in storage. It was there the review team found them years later still in the storage facility at Broadmoor. The shoes were checked against the shoeprint found near the Nickell murder and 'bingo!' a perfect match. Little did the Bisset team know on their arrest of Napper that he was wearing the same shoes he had worn when he murdered Rachel Nickell.

This chapter on forensic evidence from the Claire Tiltman murder scene can perhaps be more easily summed up by listing what was not found:

- no trace of foreign DNA either from contact with Claire, or anywhere else (with the single exception of one outstanding trace of DNA from Claire's blouse, the tests undertaken in 2013 are inconclusive, showing a mix of male and female DNA);

- no blood traces except from the victim;
- no obvious marks (except possibly Exhibit CJM/1C: above) left at or near the scene of the attack;
- nothing left behind by the attacker, i.e. cigarette butts or anything dropped in the confusion.

To sum up in one sentence: At the moment there is *no* forensic evidence. However, so long as items from a crime scene are correctly stored there is always potential. An optimistic attitude is essential to progress an enquiry. It would not be unknown, for instance, if the trace from Claire's blouse could be enhanced for it to be compared with the DNA of Colin Ash-Smith and Robert Napper, or any other suspect, whenever identified.

CHAPTER 6

Suspects Seen at or Near the Crime Scene

Police enquiries naturally went into overdrive after the murder. The investigation revealed 24 sightings of an unknown male observed at or near the murder scene at the relevant time. A composite of these sightings makes for an interesting result. It must be taken into account that as none of the sightings were positively identified they may refer to one or more individuals.

It was soon realised this was no straightforward open and shut case and the murder team set themselves up for the long haul. At 6.08 pm on Monday 18 January 1993 Danny French stepped off the Dartford to Greenhithe train at Greenhithe Railway Station. He was the last to leave the train and walked alone along Station Road towards the Railway Hotel. At the traffic lights at the junction with London Road he turned left, keeping to the left-hand side of that road, and walked up the hill on his normal route towards Knockhall Chase and his way home. French was listening to his Walkman and was changing the cassette as he approached the entrance to the alleyway which led to the doctors' surgery.

As he passed the entrance and walked on, he became aware of a young woman aged about 15 years walking down London Road towards him, further up the hill opposite the BT telephone exchange. He described her as white, about 4' 10" but possibly taller, wearing a white roll-neck top under a dark leather type waist-length jacket which was open, and her hands were tucked into the jacket's side pockets. She was also wearing black tapered trousers. Given the distance from the station to where he saw the young woman, the timing and description, this could only have been Claire Tiltman. Before she reached him, he saw a male on the same side walking a few yards in front of her. French moved to the middle of the pavement to allow the man to pass, which happened without a second thought. His description of the man was of a white male, no obvious beard or spectacles, wearing a waist-length, light-coloured jacket. The man had his hands free and wasn't carrying anything. By the way the man was walking he wasn't old and had *no distinctive limp or anything*. The last addition is a curious negative, added because by now, there was information in the system of an unidentified male with a peculiar gait or limp.

Danny French then stepped aside to allow Claire to pass, before continuing on his way home up London Road. Interestingly, French places the 'suspect' ahead of Claire just as they were opposite the entrance to Mounts Road and a very short distance from the alleyway. Without any other suspect, French found himself under scrutiny by the police. They were asking themselves, 'Why did French take that particular route home when there was a potentially shorter route available to him?' 'Why did he manage such a detailed description of Claire [there was no mention in the public notices that Claire was wearing a white roll-neck top yet] when he was very hazy about the male he saw immediately before?'.

French had contacted the incident room the very next day having recognised Claire from the publicity photograph. Police officers questioned him in depth and walked with him along the route he had taken. This exercise put the sighting of Claire near the telephone exchange in London Road at 6.15 pm. French arrived home at 6.30 pm where his mother remembered him coming in the door but noticed nothing untoward with his demeanour or clothing.

The area around Greenhithe Railway Station is in constant use with traffic and pedestrians. In the evening it is even more so as commuters return home from work and disperse from the station to their various homes. On a cold January evening nobody dallies, they are far more intent on reaching the warmth and shelter of their abodes. Claire, being a young, sociable girl was more interested in meeting her friend than hanging around in the cold. As previously explained it has never been absolutely established why Claire was in London Road which is in the opposite direction from her friend Vicky Swift's house to where Claire lived. As a packet of ten cigarettes with one missing was found in her jacket it could easily be assumed she visited the corner shop in London Road where she purchased them prior to visiting Vicky in Riverview Road. But this may be wholly wrong.

There were no witnesses found to place her in the corner shop. The shopkeeper could not remember her and there was no till receipt. One other logical reason she was in London Road was that she already had the cigarettes and was smoking one quietly in Breakneck Hill or Mounts Road before visiting Vicky where cigarettes were banned. However, without a witness to put her in the corner shop, the reason why she was in London Road must remain open. If she went into Breakneck Hill to smoke a cigarette it could account for the 'gap' in sightings as between Raymond Hurt (see later in this chapter) and Danny French. Breakneck Hill was and is a narrow lane linking Bean Road with Mounts Road overshadowed with trees and an unlikely place for any young woman to feel comfortable in after dark.

Lee Hooper, a 15-year-old schoolboy, was on his way to visit his girlfriend. He walked out of Mounts Road and then into Breakneck Hill to Bean Road where he turned left into London Road and carried on towards Stone. He saw Claire walking down the hill on the opposite side of the road and recognised her as he had met her in the British Legion Club and at karate lessons. He nodded an acknowledgement but was unsure if she returned the recognition. She didn't appear in any hurry and was behaving completely normally. As Hooper continued up the hill his attention was diverted by a noise in the direction of a field on the same side Claire was walking. He saw the figure of a man walking down the hill. The man appeared unhurried, and he could only describe him as being 5' 11" to 6' tall wearing a waist-length, dark-coloured, puffy jacket which was pulled in at the waist. At the time Hooper saw the man, the man was between 50 and 70 metres behind Claire. He did not recognise this person, nor would he have been able to identify him.

Another Lee, Lee Delguidice was also in the area, he was younger, aged 12 years. He had joined up with two friends to go to the corner shop in Knockhall Chase. He had assured his mother he would be home by 6.15 pm and checked his watch whilst waiting with two friends, James London and Stephen Westover, by the steps which lead from Station

Road up to the Greenhithe railway platforms. It was 6.08 pm and time to head for home. A very short time after this, in less than a minute, he saw a man walking from under the railway bridge in Station Road and past the telephone box. The man looked towards the boys and began to walk faster. The street lighting was very good and he saw the man clearly who he described as white, 25 to 28 years old, mid-to-dark brown hair cut short, combed forward and cut straight across at the front. Lee Delguidice thought there was something 'strange' about the man's face. 'Not angry', 'Not frightened', but pulling a face which made him look strange. He had bushy eyebrows and was 5' 8" to 5' 10" tall. He was wearing a beige or light-coloured jacket, just longer than waist-length with a zip front. It was lightweight and hung like an anorak-type coat. It was undone and flapping at his sides. He had light blue trousers and wore white training boots, not shoes.

The man continued walking quickly and looked back over his shoulder at the boys at least three times. He walked quickly on for 100 yards until he crossed the road at the first factory premises called Kent Tool DIY. He was walking as fast as if he were in a walking race. He then entered the alleyway that runs from Station Road to The Lamb public house (which is no longer there) and disappeared from view, walking in the direction of Stone Crossing Railway Station. The boys walked on from the telephone box towards the same alley and before they reached the entrance to it Delguidice heard the sound of sirens coming from the direction of London Road. This simple fact is an indicator that he had got his times slightly wrong, The first call to the ambulance service was at 6.23 pm, which puts Delguidice's sighting out by around ten minutes. He had such an uninterrupted and good view of the man he was able to tell the interviewing police officer he would recognise him again.

Kathleen Still was driving home from work and entered London Road heading towards Gravesend at 6.12 pm (This estimate was arrived at after re-driving the route later). As she drove up the hill there were no other vehicles ahead of her as she went past the alleyway on her left. As she reached the darkest part of the road she saw a man step out into the road from her right-hand side, the man paused to allow her to pass and crossed the road behind her. Still thought this strange because he crossed from a side of the road where there is no pavement or footpath, and he seemed to be talking to someone although she did not see anyone else. She describes the man as being 5' 9" to 5' 10" tall, well-built but not fat, aged 25 to 26 years with shortish light brown hair, clean shaven with 'baby-type' features. He wore a light-coloured bomber or blouson jacket of an unfashionable style. His trousers were dark, he did not wear spectacles or gloves. His expression seemed to be smiling and he stood fairly upright, looking purposeful. The man continued heading down the hill.

Christine Doyle lived in Ivy Bower Close at the end of Riverview Road which is where the doctors' surgery is situated and at the end of the alleyway which links to London Road. She was watching the six o'clock news when her attention was drawn to a man behaving oddly on the opposite side. The man had a strange walk as if he were limping or dragging his leg. He kept looking behind him, turning his head. He was walking away from the alleyway towards Riverview Road. She found it so odd she got out of her chair to have a closer view through her window. She described the man as a white, male, 5' 7" to 5' 8" tall, of ordinary build, hair not dark and not long, he was in his late thirties to early forties and wearing a light-coloured jacket like a bomber jacket but not leather or denim.

Julie Driscoll was driving along London Road towards Gravesend after finishing work. She could be accurate about the time as she remembers consulting her wristwatch. It was 6.15 pm. She was forced to stop her car behind another vehicle which was waiting to turn right into Mounts Road. She noticed a man walking down London Road on her left towards her. She described him as being of 'medium height and build', short brown hair wearing an old brown, waist-length, what appeared to be 'old leather' jacket and a pair of 'ice blue'-coloured jeans. Driscoll only had a few seconds to take this in as the man passed her and walked on down towards the traffic lights.

Rather than just carry on with a long list, I will pause here to reflect on these sightings. It may be pertinent to know that none of these witnesses were used in the forthcoming trial or appeal by Colin Ash-Smith. Why the defence ignored them is a topic for debate as we progress through the subsequent sequence of events. Suffice it to say, none of the descriptions bore a resemblance to Ash-Smith. The person to whom they did bear a resemblance will be considered later. But please bear with me. These witnesses provide an insight into who was at or near the scene at the time of the murder. Their statements were all the investigating team had to go on in the early stages of this enquiry, an enquiry which was proving to be rather difficult to solve. Of all the sightings in and around the murder scene not one of the witnesses recognised the person seen, or even less recognised him as being someone they had seen in the area on any other occasion. This fact was extremely disappointing to D Supt Taylor and his team.

The only positive that could be drawn from the failure of any witness to identify a suspect, it would appear, was that the man seen by the various witnesses was not local and was not known in Greenhithe. This would point towards the suspect not living locally. In 1993, Greenhithe wasn't as heavily populated as it is today and although one cannot say it was a small tightly knit community where everybody knew each other's business, what can be said is that there was a loose binding of locals centred on the Railway Hotel, Pier Hotel, the Sir John Franklin public houses and the Royal British Legion Club. The last of these was used by the community at large as a social club. Claire Tiltman and her parents Linda and Cliff were all members. Also, regular members there were Councillors Diane and Aubrey Ash-Smith and their son Colin.

CHAPTER 7

The Enquiry Falters

As may be imagined the tragedy of Claire's murder caused considerable upset within the community. As their only and loved child, her parents Linda and Cliff were inconsolable and could not come to terms with the loss of their lively, bright daughter. Police established, through family liaison, a close bond with the Tiltman family and the Tiltmans remained supportive of the investigation and of D Supt Taylor as the investigation teetered into the 'unsolved' category. The police now widened their investigation but, after public appeals and systematic and extensive house-to-house enquiries, they still found themselves without a viable suspect. Those on the earlier suspect list, previously mentioned, had all been eliminated.

The murder of Samantha and Jazmine Bisset was still in the future, not being committed for another ten months, on 3 November 1993. This meant that Robert Clive Napper was a completely unknown entity as far as the Tiltman enquiry was concerned, leaving a vicious stalker and murderer to carry on skulking in the shadows.

As part of house-to-house enquiries it is good practice for the investigator to note down the descriptions of those who may come within the parameters of the suspect seen in the area. For this purpose, police use a personal descriptive form (PDF). One of those for whom a PDF was completed was Colin Ash-Smith. Ash-Smith had come forward voluntarily following the police appeal for anyone who was in the area at the time and who may unwittingly have information which might link into the enquiry. Ash-Smith told police he was driving his car, a distinctive white Ford Capri with spoilers, in the area at the time. A PDF was taken and added to the list. The police had no suspicions about him other than that on his own admission he was in the area at the time of Claire's murder. This fact was not unusual as both he and his parents, local councillors Diane and Aubrey Ash-Smith, lived in the immediate vicinity. He was not even added to the growing police list of possible suspects.

As the enquiry moved on into February 1993 an approach was made to the popular BBC TV programme, *Crimewatch*. At the time this programme was at the height of its viewing figures and there was almost what could be described as a competition by police to obtain a slot on it. Due no doubt to its success, *Crimewatch* was picky over what would be included in the programme. The murder of Claire filled all the right criteria and a show was duly publicised in late February. Publicity surrounding serious crime had moved on a long way since the early days of programmes such as *Police Five* and now had productions which included actors taking the roles of victims, witnesses and perpetrators. All of which added to the piquant immediacy of the crime.

In the *Crimewatch* episode featuring the Claire Tiltman murder the presentation was introduced by Linda and Cliff Tiltman. They movingly voiced over pictures of an actor portraying Claire as a schoolgirl learning about the fire service and possibly interested in becoming a firefighter. Other performers then acted out the mundane events of her last day: leaving home, meeting friends, and arranging to meet up with her friend Vicky Swift later that evening. A mock up was made from a witness Raymond Hurt who, whilst out jogging, saw Claire walking alone down London Road towards Greenhithe from the direction of Dartford. It was misty and dark in the reconstruction and must have been a close approximation of the conditions on the evening of the attack.

Hurt's statement to the police gives rather more information than the short film clip. Having arrived home from work he changed into his running gear and went out at 5.55 pm for a run. His route took him from Kelmsley Close into Mount Road and then on to Bean Road, along Bean Road before turning into the junction with London Road. It takes approximately five minutes at jogging speed to reach the Bean Road/London Road junction which would make it 6 pm. He continued running up London Road on the southern pavement. The evening had set in and it was dark but the street lighting in London Road was good and he could see his way clearly. He saw no-one in that road until he came to the junction with Winston Close where there are two small islands in the centre of the road to facilitate traffic turning into the junction with Winston Close. At that point he saw a girl walking towards him on the same side of the road. She was aged 16 or 17, slim 5' 3"/5' 4" wearing black shoes and trousers and a dark, below waist-length jacket. This person without any doubt was Claire Tiltman. He estimates the time of seeing Claire within one minute to 6.10 pm.

Raymond Hurt continued jogging to the doctors' surgery in Woodward Terrace where he picked up a prescription. There was no queue and no delay and he left the surgery to run the reverse route home. He ran back down London Road on the same south side as before and, as he was about 200 yards from the Bean Road junction, he again saw Claire. She was walking in front of him on the same path and as he was about to overtake her near the traffic lights she moved to the outside of the pavement forcing him to take a wider berth. He was faintly annoyed but continued running and did not see where Claire had gone as he turned into Bean Road and continued on his running route until he reached his home.

Another witness, Paul Harris, driving up London Road with his girlfriend Gitte Hansen saw a young woman rush out from the alleyway leading to Riverview Road and into the main London Road. The young woman was waving her arms and looking back up the alleyway. Hansen felt the girl was 'in panic' but that she was laughing and probably having horseplay with friends.

It seems to have been only afterwards when Harris heard the news of what had actually happened that he revised his opinion to believing the girl was screaming. He had seen a car parked half on and half off the pavement at the traffic lights in a very dangerous position. Not realising the significance of the young woman, who was fleeing from an attack, he drove on. Harris glanced in his rear view mirror and saw Claire leaning over the low brick wall. These were the last moments of Claire's life.

The events of Michael Godfrey and Ron Wilson discovering Claire slumped next to a wall and then the arrival of the ambulance crew was acted out. More family background was filled in with Linda and Cliff

Tiltman describing how they would visit the British Legion Club in Greenhithe and how Claire was adept at playing pool. Linda Tiltman then made an impassioned plea for the murderer to come forward and hand 'himself' in. She concluded her address with the statement, 'Maybe he is capable of doing it again.'

D Supt Owen Taylor then did a face-to-face interview with the presenter Nick Ross. He underlined his fear that the attacker could in all likelihood strike again. He was convinced the perpetrator either lived in or had connections to the area. He was also convinced that someone would know or suspect who the killer was.

In these public interviews it is a fine balance as to how much information to divulge. Too much and it may be to the detriment of any future interview with a suspect. It may prepare the suspect for what to expect or on another tangent it may provide information to that peculiar set of individuals who wish, through their own misguided attempts at notoriety, to make a fake confession. In this instance D Supt Taylor decided to release the fact that a large knife was used, and that Claire was stabbed several times. It had been established that the murder weapon was of the hunting knife variety and no ordinary penknife.

The number of times Claire was stabbed was also of interest. It had entered into the public notion that she was stabbed many times, a figure which gradually increased in the telling to over 40. In fact, Claire had been stabbed nine times. Finally, further reference was made to the vehicle seen parked askew at the traffic lights. A picture was shown of a nondescript grey hatchback parked at the junction with its lights on.

An appearance on *Crimewatch* can produce spectacular results; unfortunately, it didn't in this case, only a further long list of possible suspects and misleading information from sometimes well-meaning members of the public and sometimes from people using the programme as a vehicle for their own vindictive ends. It may be said that an appeal to *Crimewatch* is a sign that an enquiry is running out of steam and desperation is creeping in. Suspects were cropping up and were being eliminated. The appeal for the public to come forward with any information no matter how trivial prompted a massive response but with time the information inevitably started to dry up.

There were several sightings of an unrecognised male at or near the scene just before or after the murder. The most significant sighting which appears to be just after the killing was from the previously mentioned Christine Doyle, who saw a man outside the window of her house in Ivy Bower Close. That house is situated a few doors down from the doctors' surgery in Ivy Bower Close and almost opposite the exit of the alleyway leading from London Road. Her sighting is a very interesting view of a male behaving in Mrs Doyle's words 'oddly' and moving away from the alleyway.

The Riverview Road end of the alleyway has two exits. One is at the end of the alleyway, which leads up from London Road and turns sharp right exiting into Ivy Bower Close between the houses. There is another exit half way up the alleyway which leads up a steep set of stone steps and emerges opposite the doctors' surgery. This exit provides a prefect hiding place within the alleyway, the exit being concealed by large bushes. It remains the same now as it did then. Witnesses saw Claire dash from the alleyway and collapse in London Road next to the low wall, which also remains and is now covered with a flower bed in her memory, together with a commemorative plaque.

The witness Diane Eversfield saw Claire stagger out of the alleyway into London Road looking over her shoulder. This would indicate Claire had been attacked in the alleyway, broke free and made it to the London Road exit. Her injuries were so severe that she could not possibly have travelled more than a few strides before collapsing. There was also what was thought to be arterial blood spattering on the last wood panelled fencing next to the London Road exit. That fence was on the right-hand side as you look down the alleyway towards the London Road. The left side is framed by a concrete wall. No blood was found on the wall. The wooden part of the fence that the blood was on was removed by police for more detailed examination. Despite further tests the blood could not conclusively be proved to be Claire's, because of contamination. The best that could be established by scientist Roger Mann was that it was human blood.

The indications are that Claire was walking through the alleyway towards Ivy Bower Close when she was attacked by someone concealed in the exit by the surgery steps. Most stabbing blows were to her front right chest area. Pathologist Dr Heath's report suggests that the first blow, which he labelled as No. 7 (not the seventh wound) struck just to the left of her sternum. All of the other chest wounds were to her right front chest. She turned and fled back towards the main road pursued by her attacker, who stabbed her again in the right side of her back puncturing an arterial blood vessel and, upon withdrawing the knife, blood sprayed onto the fence. Dr Heath referred to this wound as 'Blow One'. It entered through her fourth and fifth ribs. The blade passed behind her spine and ruptured her 'descending thoracic artery'.

Having reached the main road, Claire was not followed and whoever had attacked her must have retreated back into the alleyway and exited into Ivy Bower Close via one of the two exits described above. This is where he was seen by Christine Doyle who gave a very good description of the man seen from her window. The timing of this sighting wasn't tightened during her statement, merely saying that she was interrupted whilst watching the six o'clock news. No question was asked about what item of news was interrupted which would have given a more accurate time. However, it was established that the dark unlit alleyway was infrequently used during the hours of darkness and the suspicious male seen by Mrs Doyle was walking towards the railway station.

It is highly likely this man was Claire's killer. She described the male as white 5' 7"/5' 8". He was of medium build wearing a light-coloured jacket. The man appeared to be limping or 'dragging' his leg. His curious behaviour included constantly looking over his shoulder toward the alleyway entrance. She described the man as 'walking away from the doctors' surgery.' This is an important point as it would suggest the man she saw had come from the middle exit of the alleyway, in other words the point from where Claire was likely to have been attacked. The suspect moved away from Mrs Doyle's house and walked purposefully away, down the hill, in the direction of Greenhithe Railway Station. Subsequent enquiries at the doctors' surgery gave no indication of anyone attending there who answered Mrs Doyle's description of the man she saw in Ivy Bower Close.

Before we leave the crime scene it is worth taking a look at the blood distribution coupled with Claire's injuries. This becomes highly significant later in the enquiry. Although I have attended scores of murder scenes, I cannot claim to be a blood spatter analyst. However I have enough experience through working with experts to be able to form an opinion albeit not an expert one in the technical sense. If Claire's attacker was hiding by the doctors' surgery steps and jumped out and attacked her as she approached, the stab wounds to her right side would indicate a right-handed assailant. (Just try and go through the motions using your left hand).

The final blow from behind which sprayed blood onto the fence on the right side again would show the knife being plunged and withdrawn by a right-handed person as he chased the victim towards London Road. This must be borne in mind as later events in this book unfold. Suffice it to say that no observations as to the 'handedness' (left or right) of the assailant were made at the first post mortem by Dr Heath and so far as can be established no opinion was sought at that time.

As a result of the police appeal and extensive media coverage many witnesses came forward to describe cars and suspicious males in the vicinity both before and after the murder. One of those who voluntarily came forward was Colin Ash-Smith. Ash-Smith lived with his parents Diane and Aubrey in Milton Street in nearby Swanscombe. He was an only child and well-known locally. It is worth underlining that both of his parents were heavily involved in the local community, both being councillors, Diane even becoming Mayor of Greenhithe and Swanscombe. They both took their community duties very seriously.

Colin was born in and had lived all of his life in the area. He had a love of motor cars and was never seen far away from his pride and joy the white Ford Capri which was complete with the usual 'boy racer' accoutrements including a 'whale tail spoiler' on the boot. A car which stood out and was instantly recognisable.

Ash-Smith contacted the incident room the day after the murder at 10 am on Tuesday 19 January. After giving his details he told the receiving officer he was driving towards Dartford past the British Legion in Greenhithe at about 6.30 pm when, at the zebra crossing, he saw a male using the crossing. He only 'glanced' at this person and could not describe him further other than he had dark curly hair.

On January 25, Ash-Smith made a formal statement to police. He described himself as a lifting gear specialist and he gave a description of his Ford Capri, then an account of what he saw on the evening of Monday 18 January. According to Ash-Smith he was driving his Capri at between 17.45 and 17.55 (a significant discrepancy from the time of 18.30 given in his initial PDF report) in London Road, Greenhithe heading in the direction of Dartford. As he passed the Esso filling station, on his left side, he saw a figure which he was unable to categorise as either male or female walking towards Dartford on his left side. This person he described as 5' 6" to 5' 8" aged 20 to 30 with long shoulder-length hair straight on top and wavy at the bottom. He went on to mention that his mother Diane Ash-Smith was with him in the car.

When asked later, Mrs Ash-Smith had no recollection of the person Colin described. Colin claims to have turned left into Knockhall Chase and driven on to Eynsford Road where his mother was delivering a letter on council business to an elderly resident, Edward (Ted) Wells, who resided there. It was not an unusual event for Colin to drive his mother about locally assisting her with her council tasks. At this time she could not drive.

He waited outside the house sitting in his car for his mother to deliver the letter, which took only a matter of moments. He then drove back home with her to Milton Street, taking an alternative route through Greenhithe avoiding the London Road. They arrived home at approximately 6 pm where he stayed for the remainder of the evening. Ash-Smith mentions in this statement that he knew the Tiltman family because they and his family were members of the British Legion Club. He had occasionally played pool with Claire in the club.

A month later on February 25, Colin Ash-Smith was asked to make a further statement to expand on his knowledge of the Tiltman family. The request for the statement incidentally was made on the same day as Claire's funeral, which Colin, Diane and Aubrey all attended. He had been a member of the British Legion Club for five years. He knew the Tiltman family as regular members of the club and was on first name terms with them. He also knew Claire, with whom he would play pool. He described her as a good player who would often play with her father. One or the other of her parents would always accompany Claire to the club and Colin had no other contact with her socially.

Ash-Smith went on to explain that after taking his mother home to Milton Street on the night of the murder he remained indoors all evening with her. His father Aubrey was at home when he arrived with his mother but left shortly afterwards to go to the British Legion Club. Colin Ash-Smith fell asleep on the settee until he was woken by the return of his father at 10.30 pm, who told his mother he had heard of a stabbing that evening in Greenhithe. It wasn't until the following morning that Colin heard on the radio that the victim was Claire Tiltman and, as a result, contacted the police to declare he had been in the vicinity with his mother.

Neither Aubrey nor Diane Ash-Smith were asked to make statements to the police. Colin was as far from being a suspect as anyone could be. It wasn't until three years later, after Colin had been arrested for the attack on Charlotte Barnard, that they were asked to make statements concerning their movements on the night of Claire's murder. In Aubrey's statement dated 22 November 1995 he says he got back home at 11.30 pm. Diane's statement dated 24 November 1995 states Aubrey returned home at about 11 pm. Not a very well thought out 'conspiracy.'

Colin Ash-Smith's unremarkable witness statement was added to the growing pile of those recording the evidence of individuals who had seen or might have seen something. Whoever the figure was who he claimed to have seen by the zebra crossing it was unlikely to have been Claire as she was well-known to him ... Unless the whole statement was a fabrication.

CHAPTER 8

Events Outside Kent

As the Kent investigation moved on into increasingly labyrinthine territory, and as investigators extended their enquiry, other offences elsewhere were coming into sharper focus.

In the spring of 1992, a series of increasingly violent sexually motivated attacks on women had been happening in south east London. The one certain fact about this particular string of offences was that they were all indisputably committed by the same perpetrator. At four of the crime scenes the suspect left behind forensic evidence in the form of DNA which showed without doubt that the offences were committed by the same person. Unfortunately for the police the database of DNA samples was a fraction of what it is today and nowhere on that system was there a name to correspond with these DNA samples. Although, the DNA sample did match that of a suspect for a rape in 1989 in a house in Purret Road, Plumstead adjacent to Winns Common where a young mother had been raped by an intruder who had gained access via the rear door of the house which backed onto a garden next to the common.

The attacker had ignored the victim's children who were eating their breakfast downstairs, climbed the stairs and raped the woman in her bedroom. When finished, he calmly walked back past the children and made his escape through the garden and then across the common. The DNA captured at this crime scene matched that from the spree of attacks which happened along the Green Chain Walk during 1992. Strangely the modus operandi (MO) of the rape in 1989 bore little similarity to the string of attacks in 1992. With one major exception the attacker did not appear to be deterred from attacking women who were in the presence of small children.

The series of rapes on the Green Chain Walk in 1992 are dealt with in greater depth elsewhere so it is not my intention here to go into them in too much detail.[3] After the Purret Road incident in 1989 and the securing of a DNA sample which was safely logged in police records awaiting a match, the same sexual predator struck again, this time on 10 March 1992 on the Cordwell Estate, London SE13. At the time Robert Napper was living about two miles away in Well Hall Road, Eltham. The Cordwell Estate area is well built up and the victim was walking alone to visit a friend when at 8.45 pm as she approached an alleyway leading from Northbrook Road to the Cordwell Estate she noticed a man ten yards behind her walking in the same direction on the opposite side of the road. By this time of the evening in early March the sun had set, and it was dark as she entered the alleyway. When she had covered three quarters of its length, she heard the sound of footsteps running up behind her. Suddenly feeling vulnerable she looked over her shoulder and saw the same man she had seen earlier, walking only five yards behind her.

The woman increased her pace and reached the end of the alleyway which exited into a small yard. As she did so the man ran towards some lock up garages on her right. She was seriously alarmed now and hurried into the next alleyway. Before she knew what was happening, she was grabbed by her right arm by the same man who was now holding a knife in his right hand which he pointed close to and at her stomach. The man spoke aggressively, 'If you want to live don't make any noise.' He dragged her back to the garages trying to kiss her mouth which she resisted. He ordered her to undo her jacket and she again refused. His reaction was to force up her clothing and viciously grab her breasts. At the slightest sign of resistance, he laid the knife against her stomach and said, 'Shut up. If you want to live, be quiet.'

Without warning he punched her three or four times hard on her left cheek causing her head to smash against the garage wall. He pulled down her jeans and underwear and attempted to rape her but could not raise an erection. Just as quickly as he had started, he stopped. As if distracted, he looked to one side and then stood up. Again, without

---

3. See *Napper: Through A Glass Darkly*, Waterside Press (2019).

warning, he kicked her head and continued kicking for six or seven blows as she attempted to shield herself. Without saying another word, the man walked off. The victim staggered the few yards to her friend's house where the alarm was raised.

This first rape in what was to become the Green Chain Rapes series (given the name Operation Eccleston) bears many similarities to the Claire Tiltman murder. One can immediately cross-reference the MO, beloved of detectives real and fictional. However, care must be taken in applying too much emphasis to an MO. Obviously it is a tool in the detective's armoury but consider: we know beyond any shadow of doubt that the 'monster' who attacked this innocent young woman was Robert Napper. The study in isolation of the MO used at the attack on the Cordwell Estate does contain similarities to the Tiltman attack but there are also anomalies. There was no actual use of the knife, only threats. There is only an implied sexual assault on Claire Tiltman whereas the first in this series was centred entirely, if unsuccessfully, on the sexual act. Remember also, this is the first of the series. Police will link it quickly to the 1989 rape in the house in Purret Road, Plumstead but they do not know Robert Napper, he is completely off their radar. Beware of 'hindsight bias'.

The victim of the rape described her attacker in the following terms. A white male aged about 20 years, 5' 8" tall of stocky build and dark brown straight hair, brown eyes and a clear complexion, he spoke with a south east London accent. He was wearing blue jeans and a brown bomber jacket.

Eight days later on 18 March 1992 the rapist struck again. This time on more open land but still at around the same time, 8 pm. The attack happened on a public footpath, King John's Walk, which runs between open fields on the outskirts of Eltham, south east London. The young woman victim was walking southwards on the footpath towards Mottingham. She had walked the route many times before and despite the darkness and lack of street lighting felt safe. She heard footsteps coming up quickly behind her and turned to see a man catching up with her. She dropped her eyes to avoid eye contact as the man passed her. There was something about the man which made her feel uncomfortable, so she stopped and began to walk back toward the walls of Eltham Palace. Looking backwards she could see the figure of the man disappearing down the lane. At this point she made a fateful decision and decided to cut across Vista Field (so called because of a spectacular view of London in the far distance) and take an unmade track which she knew was a short cut to her parents' house, but, at that time of the evening, dark and isolated. She hadn't gone far along the footpath when she was suddenly confronted by the man who had passed her earlier and who must have circled around to place himself in front of her.

The man was holding a six-inch bladed knife in his right hand and wearing a balaclava but with his face partly showing. Using an odd pattern of speech he said to her, 'Get down on your knees. I've got this. I'll use it. I'm not going to hurt you. I'm not going to screw you. I just want to put my tongue in your mouth. I want to kiss you.' He forced her backwards and pressed the knife up against her breast. He forced up her jumper and bra and having stripped her of her lower clothing attempted unsuccessfully to rape her. When he eventually stopped, he placed the point of the knife on her body and moved it up and down between her breasts and chin. He said, 'You could have got this.' He stood up and walked off in the direction of King John's Walk whilst she made good her escape in the opposite direction to raise the alarm.

The police took the following description. The man was white, about 5' 7" tall. Aged about 19 years he had brown mousy hair. The oddest thing about him was the way he spoke, as if he were in an interview, pronouncing his words slowly and carefully. The victim when examined was found to have a small puncture wound made by the knife in her left breast. Analysis of seminal fluid on the victim's clothing showed a DNA profile which matched that of the earlier attack in the Cordwell Estate. The police had a serial rapist on their hands.

An incident room was set up in Eltham Police Station under the command of D Supt Steve Landeryou, a detective of the old school with a long record of murder investigations. He was in the twilight of his career and favoured the quiet life, preferring I think to dwell on past glories. In this particular investigation it was only going to be a matter of time before the protagonist was going to come to light through the new science of DNA... Wasn't it?

Applying hindsight bias again, it must again be remembered that the use of DNA evidence in criminal trials was in its infancy. The science itself was far from the sleek model we take for granted over 30 years later. The laboratory required a significant deposit of semen or blood before attempting to raise a profile. The idea of obtaining profiles from such items as cigarette butts or sweat traces was still far in the future. This coupled with reluctance from the judiciary to accept DNA evidence as a legitimate tool in identifying individuals was also very much in its trial stage within the courts.

The first ever conviction of murder relying on DNA evidence was not until the case of Colin Pitchfork in September 1987. Pitchfork had raped and murdered two children, one in November 1983 the other in July 1986. The first murder predated DNA and relied upon blood-typing and enzymes, the sample of which matched 10% of the population. After the second murder police had access to DNA and were able to prove that the incriminating evidence left at the scene matched Pitchfork and also the sample retained from the 1983 offence, demonstrating that, far from a 10% chance of the producer of both samples being the offender, it was millions to one against it *not* being him. The trial went ahead and against a spirited attempt by the defence to discredit DNA Pitchfork was found guilty. The foundation for the use of DNA evidence in criminal trials was firmly established.

This is more than a little poignant as, in the headlong rush to defend the rights of Pitchfork, another man, a youngster with some learning difficulties called Richard Buckland had been arrested for and had admitted the second murder in a police interview, but consistently denied the first murder. Modern knowledge of DNA clearly demonstrates that if Buckland had not committed the second offence, he could not have committed the first. No doubt, prior to the development of DNA, Buckland would have found himself convicted of both murders on the strength of his (false) confession to the second. The Buckland incident has some parallels to the Tiltman case which will be drawn into focus later.

It is perfectly understandable why such resistance should be in place. Matters of vital importance need testing in court to their utmost limits. The fact that the legal profession may have some sort of legal stake in non-acceptance of such evidence is incidental. Similar resistance occurred a century earlier when the use of fingerprint evidence was introduced and it took many years before being totally accepted by the courts. Although a DNA database had Home Office approval, by 1993 it was still in the early stages of forming a comprehensive stockpile of DNA samples to compare against possible suspects. Couple this with the fact that police still did not have the power to routinely take a DNA sample from every prisoner. This even went so far as to result in the introduction of a directive that no sample could be taken from those who had committed an offence unless it reached the 'serious' category. The 'direction' was loosely worded and did not clarify what the word 'serious' meant, choosing to leave it open to interpretation.

Hence, Napper did not have his DNA taken when he was arrested and found guilty of a firearms offence and of being in possession of a 'section one' firearm and ammunition without a firearms certificate. This was in October 1992 and was not considered enough to cross the threshold to take a DNA sample. Had this been done he would have immediately been identified as the Green Chain Rapist thereby preventing the murders of Samantha and Jazmine Bisset and maybe others. So, before any reader leaps to the defence of the human right to privacy, bear that fact in mind and ask yourself, 'What would have been Samantha Bisset's views on Napper's rights to privacy?' The law surrounding the taking of DNA samples by police has, after a long struggle, now been widened to include all those who enter into police custody.

Another skill taken for granted by current investigators but in its infancy in 1992 was geographic profiling. Napper was dismissed out of hand by the Tiltman investigating team, their main reasoning being the belief that theirs was a 'Kent' job. Whatever Napper had been up to, it certainly didn't impinge on their investigation. Parochialism is a common scourge in investigating major crime and persists to this day. Petty jealousies and historic enmities can go a long way to preventing the smooth running of an investigation once it runs over what are only boundary lines on an arbitrary map. To be fair to the Kent investigators, they had little intimate knowledge of the Nickell murder and it bore little similarity on the face of it to the murder of Claire Tiltman. In their eyes, Greenhithe was the centre of operations and it was one of the biggest murder investigations Kent had ever managed.

No one murder is any more 'important' than any other. The taking of a life and its subsequent investigation is at the forefront of police investigation. However, some crimes touch the public and the police conscience more than others. It would have been a difficult concept for the Kent police investigators to contemplate that Claire's murder could have been on the fringe of an even larger and much more far-reaching enquiry.

Napper, having evaded the request to provide a sample for a DNA comparison, had hurriedly moved to a bedsit at 63 Reidhaven Road, Plumstead. After his short spell in prison, at the end of 1992 on his release he moved back to 63 Reidhaven Road where he stayed until early April 1993. So when Claire and Jean Bradley were killed in January and March 1993 respectively he was living at that address (before moving to 135 Plumstead High Street in April 1993).

Even in his deranged state of mind Napper must have been expecting a follow up call from the police. He must also have been wondering if the police had joined up the dots and linked him to the murder of Rachel Nickell. He need not have worried. As far as the police were concerned, he was an insignificant nobody of little or no interest to anybody. As he brooded in his well-kept but tiny bedsit, his increasingly psychotic mind was dreaming of further offences. Offences he planned in his *A to Z* of London streets and on sheets of notepaper where he reflected, by drawing cryptic images of past attacks and current possibilities. He sank into a world of self-delusion, believing he was a hero of the Angolan war. He was on the hit list of the IRA. He knew the queen personally and was in receipt of the Nobel Peace Prize. All these delusions were kept firmly locked within his own diseased mind and not shared with anyone.

He kept up his training regime, walking for hours through woodlands and along the Green Chain Walk, fantasising about attacking vulnerable women. He became obsessed with weaponry, going on a day trip to France where he bought a .22 pistol and smuggled it back into England.

He purchased a crossbow, something that was found in the search of his flat after his arrest for attempting to copy Metropolitan Police headed notepaper. He also started in earnest to purchase, via magazine adverts, what were described as weapons of defence but, in reality, weapons with which to commit extreme and fatal violence, mainly based on military designs. Napper was by now presenting a sexual psychodrama. It had a pattern but was adjustable to circumstances and events.

As he walked out of the front door of his bedsit and climbed anonymously down the Victorian steps he would have quickly worked out he was only five minutes walk from Plumstead Railway Station. Familiar as he was with the use of public transport, he would also have found that a train, Kent bound, leaves every half hour. This regular commuter service stops at every station and takes exactly 21 minutes from Plumstead to arrive in the old coastal town of Greenhithe.

On 24 May 1992 another assault happened in the same location, King John's Walk Eltham. On this occasion the assailant veered away again from what may have been considered Napper's MO. The attack was in broad daylight at 2 pm and the young female victim had her two-year-old daughter with her in a pushchair going from Eltham towards Mottingham. Ahead of her in the distance she saw the figure of a man cross the footpath from her right to the left. Unconcerned she walked purposefully on, enjoying a country walk with her daughter. She passed the spot where she had seen the figure cross the path and within a few moments heard footsteps behind her. Before she had a chance to turn, she felt something pass over her head and suddenly she was jerked backwards as a ligature tightened around her neck. She instinctively grabbed the cord and let go of the buggy. A voice told her to put her hands behind her back, she complied and the pressure on the cord was relaxed.

The woman pleaded with her attacker to release her, 'Because of my little girl.' All this achieved was for her to be roughly told to 'shut up', and being thrown onto her back. The attacker tried to remove her upper clothing but she resisted. He then removed her shorts and underwear, attempting as in previous assaults and failing to complete the sex act. During the assault the victim, although she had little recollection of the sequence of events, was later found to be suffering from blows to the head and body which had been inflicted with 'considerable force.' Again, without warning the attacker stood up, pulled up his old-fashioned Y fronts and shorts and walked off towards Eltham. The victim like the others was pitilessly abandoned. She made her painful way with her child to her mother-in-law's house, where the crime was reported to the police and she was conveyed to hospital. At the hospital she was briefly questioned by a constable in uniform who asked how tall she thought the attacker was. The reply would prove significant and a thorn in the side of the investigation for evermore. To recap about the strange way in which the suspect's height was estimated, as described in *Chapter 4*. The officer said, 'Was he as tall as me? I'm 6' 3".' To which she replied, 'Yeah. About your height.' Later when the victim came to make a written statement her description of her attacker was white, slim with short brown hair, aged 26 to 30 years. He had dirty grey teeth and a spotty chin. He was wearing a t-shirt, blue shorts and grey socks. Crucially she also estimated his height as being about 5' 7". How this discrepancy in height estimates occurred has never been satisfactorily explained. What is without doubt is that, when the DNA results came back, they matched the previous rapes and it confirmed that all the offences were committed by the same attacker. An attacker we in the world of hindsight now know to be Robert Clive Napper.

Operation Eccleston had suddenly become a very high-profile case. The timing coincided with another innovative tool in the fight against crime. A technique which was named 'psychological profiling'. It would, by the time these investigations had panned out, become a byword for notoriety and heavy-handed police work. The system had been enthusiastically taken up by the nationwide Association of Chief Police Officers (ACPO) who saw it as the future in criminal investigation. The fall out from its use in the sequence of events which followed would set the practice back 20 years. Psychological profiling was in its infancy when it impacted on the Green Chain Rapes, the murder of Rachel Nickell, and of Samantha and Jazmine, as well as being considered for the Claire Tiltman case. The first three were all to be analysed by the same psychological profiler, Paul Britton, who also had an input into the Tiltman investigation. Before considering psychological profiling, thought should be given to an important evidential factor in all these cases, i.e. eye-witness descriptions of suspects and eye-witness identification.

As can be seen from the descriptions provided by Napper's rape victims, even though we now know the attacks were all committed by the same individual the descriptions varied quite considerably. This is hardly surprising for some offences happened in poor lighting and in one offence he wore a balaclava. This coupled with the shock and disorientation the victims were under makes it understandable. There are many discrepancies in the descriptions, from spotty to clear skin, from 19 to 30 years, there is also a difference in clothing on each occasion, which may of course be a fact. One offence occurred without any sign of a knife being used. On another a height difference from 5' 7" to 6' 3". It can be seen that without DNA evidence proving they were one and the same man it would be difficult to arrive at the same conclusion. However, utilising the descriptions they had, the police produced a Photofit, constructed from all the witnesses. It was this Photofit, coupled with his bizarre behaviour, which led to Napper's neighbours and a work colleague naming him to Operation Eccleston, the Green Chain Rapes squad. This started a sequence of events which will go down in history as a police bungle and led not only to the Green Chain Rapist not being summarily caught, but the subsequent murders of three innocents. And, as we shall see, possibly more.

But is the tag 'bungle' a fair epithet to apply to the rape investigation. As we have seen, identification evidence is unreliable. In this case such evidence was not needed to present to the court because the investigating team at this stage did not have a suspect. They did however have an artist's impression. An impression, which consequently turned out to be uncannily accurate, although, as it relied on the accumulated descriptions of more than one witness, the investigators were not able to totally rely upon its accuracy.

As the summer of 1992 drifted on towards autumn, there was a sudden and unexplained cessation of attacks on women on the Green Chain Walk. The artist's impression had been widely published and as already noted the case had achieved a spot on the BBC TV show *Crimewatch*. At about this time the use of psychological profilers was becoming a tool in the investigator's armoury. Studies in the United States of America coupled with some spectacular successes led ACPO to encourage and promulgate their use in the United Kingdom. This coincided with a popular fictional TV show of the time called *Cracker* starring the late Robbie Coltrane. The whole conspired for the application of the techniques involved to be applied to high-profile undetected cases of murder. This coincided with the early successes of DNA profiling. Undoubtedly in some chief police officers minds the mixture of the possibilities of psychological profiling and the fictional variety became conflated.

At the forefront of this innovative new way of assisting an investigation was consultant clinical psychologist Paul Britton. A man who had studied the FBI's methods and already had had some success assisting the police in the UK. A summary of his work is to be found in his book *The Jigsaw Man*.[4] Britton was asked to contact the Green Chain Rape team at Eltham, which he did, and after studying the case he produced a psychological profile of the offender. He concluded that the offender would (paraphrased):

- Be aged between 18 and 24 but was unlikely to be over 28.
- Be of low to average intelligence, unlikely to have performed well academically.
- If employed, have work that was undemanding intellectually.
- Work maybe in a group, but he would shun women colleagues.
- Any women friends would be much younger, less threatening, more easily impressed.
- Be a reckless risk-taker, who, whilst offending was relatively unconcerned about apprehension.
- Derive satisfaction from the fear he produced in his victims.
- Clearly from his offence style, interaction (viz certain victim responses) be such that the situation *could lead to the death of the victim* (my emphasis).
- Express considerable rage and anger (There were indications he was taunting police).

4. Paul Britton, *The Jigsaw Man*, Corgi (New edn. 1998).

- Be likely to be known to police covering the areas of the assaults.
- Possibly be a burglar.
- Have connections to the area by residence, schooling and employment.
- Possibly have moved away between the first [Purrett Road, Plumstead] and second [Cordwell Estate, SE13] offence.
- Be expected to be suffering from the following: (1) sexual deviant fantasy; (2) sexual dysfunction; erectile problems, premature ejaculation; (3) inability to sustain heterosexual relationships.
- Have victims who could be regarded as having similar signs of 'vulnerability' although little by way of physical similarity.
- Bring himself to attention in one of three ways: (1) by information provided by the public or area police officers; (2) being caught during an offence; (3) by an elimination process based upon examination of records.
- Be dangerous and would continue to offend and might escalate his violence according to victim reaction.

This is a very comprehensive study and incredibly accurate when compared to the offender, a man we now know to be Robert Napper.

The provision of this type of profile was extremely innovative at the time. Naturally it did meet with its detractors, even from within the ranks of the investigators. I have heard these profiles described as 'obvious' or 'the conclusion which any rational investigator may arrive at'. It can be seen that profiling could attract polar opposite viewpoints, from the dismissive to the idealistic and slavish approach seemingly taken by the Nickell investigators. It must be remembered that when the profile was submitted to Operation Eccleston, Napper wasn't even in their 'comprehensive' HOLMES system. He was still in the shadows, moving around without any hint of suspicion drawn to him. Seen by everyone yet seen by no-one.

A sequence of events then took place, which, not for the first time and not the last, allowed Napper to slip through the net. Despite all of the effort expended on Operation Eccleston the offender had not been identified and also had not apparently committed any offences since the last known rape on 24 May 1992. So, by August of that year there was pressure to close down Operation Eccleston. We look back with horror now, knowing that Napper attacked and murdered Rachel Nickell on the 15 July 1992. However, the Eccleston enquiry team had no reason to link the rape offences to a 'wild' murder over 20 miles away on the opposite side of London. Even in the soft glow of hindsight, they were however a little overeager to shut down the investigation.

On the 19 August 1992 (one month after the murder of Rachel Nickell) a woman was walking across Woolwich Common to the bus stop in Academy Road. She reached it and was waiting alone for a bus when she was approached by a man she described as white, 5' 9" tall, slim build with short medium brown hair parted on the left. Aged 25 to 30 years with a grubby, long, pockmarked face, staring eyes and 'sad' lips, he was wearing a bright red t-shirt and blue jeans cut off at the knee. His speech was curiously pronounced as he spoke in a London accent through dirty, uneven teeth. He asked the woman if it was permitted to walk up Academy Road. She replied it was and he walked off in the direction of Eltham.

Feeling disturbed by the encounter, the woman continued to stand alone at the bus stop when, after a few minutes, she saw the same man walking back towards her. He stood next to her at the bus stop and entered into conversation in a peculiar staccato manner.

'You can't walk up the hill.'

'Why not? she replied.

'There are dead bodies up there. Someone has been dragged to their death.'

Feeling ever more perturbed as the man drew closer to her, she was relieved to see a bus approaching. Even though it wasn't the one she was waiting for, she took the opportunity and boarded it. The man stayed on the footpath until the very last moment and then jumped onto the bus as the doors were closing. She was uncomfortably aware of him staring at her as the bus continued its way up the hill towards the crossroads of Shooters Hill and Woolwich Road.

These crossroads carry a powerful historic feel as they were once on the main road from London to Dover and a favourite haunt of highwaymen as they attacked coaches entering the thick woodland of Oxleas Wood. So notorious a spot was it, that a gibbet had been erected at the crossroads to display the rotting corpses of unsuccessful robbers as a deterrent to others. Although the gibbet was long gone there remained an old police station which in 1992 was still operational. The area was still covered heavily in ancient oak woodland, some of which would have stood witness to the long-departed gibbet.

As the bus came to a stop outside the police station the woman bolted from it using the front 'entry door'. To her further alarm she saw the man also alight from the bus. She walked quickly and purposefully towards the police station which seemed to deter her pursuer as she watched him run off across the common and disappear into the woods behind what was then the Welcome Inn public house.

There are some interesting facts about this incident. The man was Robert Napper and we know this because after his arrest in 1994 the woman identified him without any doubt in an identity parade. Napper at the time was living in Well Hall Road, very close to the Welcome Inn. When interviewed by police about this troubling incident the woman told them that the man bore a close resemblance to the Photofit for the Green Chain Rapist which was in wide circulation at the time. The timing of the would-be attack provokes more questions.

The Woolwich bus incident was at 6 pm on 19 August 1992. The last known rape, which was in King John's Walk, Eltham was at 2 pm on the 24 May 1992 (I will include the year in all references to aid comprehension). As far as the police were aware no other offences had taken place between 24 May and 19 August 1992. We now know that Napper had travelled over 20 miles across London and on the morning of the 15 July 1992 had murdered Rachel Nickell on Wimbledon Common. An offence committed between the last known Green Chain Rape and the woman accosted at the Shooters Hill bus stop.

Rather than use the benefit of hindsight to crudely batter police, highlighting their 'failings', consider what this now tells us of the behaviour of Napper. With the passage of time we naturally lose some evidence, but we also gain something not gifted to the investigator at the time, a completely new perspective, fuelled with (unknown at the time) indisputable facts. We know without doubt that whilst living in Well Hall Road, Eltham, Napper violently attacked three women between 10 March and 24 May 1992. The attacks were all sexually motivated. Two of them were committed on late, dark winter evenings. The other attack was at 2 pm in broad daylight. All attacks were committed in the open on public pathways, some more secluded than others. Two of the offences (if we include that on Rachel Nickell and the final King John's Walk attack) were carried out in the presence of young children, both of whom seemed to have had no restraining effect on the assailant.

How can it be credible that Napper, after his series of rapes and then murdering Rachel Nickell, did not commit any further offences for another 16 months until the murders of the Bissets in November 1993? We know now that only one month after the murder of Rachel he was lining up another victim, who had a fortunate escape, in Woolwich Road close to his address. It is simply unbelievable.

I have heard theories of how, after the murder of Rachel Nickell, Napper was somehow sated for a time, a cruel fulfilment which deterred him from the need to attack again until, after a gradual build up, he burst forth in violent mayhem at the Bisset murders 16 months later.

The Woolwich bus incident only one month after Rachel's murder completely undermines this theory. The police had no firm evidence to link this incident to their Green Chain Rapes enquiry, still less to consider Rachel Nickell as one of Napper's victims. I am no apologist for the police and am merely stating the facts. What cannot be ignored is that police had received information that Napper could be considered as a suspect for the rapes, and he was asked to provide a specimen to compare against an unknown offender—and despite two ignored requests he was eliminated from the enquiry by the supervising officers as being 'too tall' to fit the 'known' parameters.

APJ/17

1

VISITORS

DATE	NAME
19/1/93	Dartford Incident Room BBC Camera Crews Skye Camera Crews. Meridian Camera Crews.
20/1/93	Dartford Incident Room BBC Camera Crew.
22/1/93	MR. CONDON Chief Constable Chief Inspector Philpott Staff Office
25/1/93	H. W. Mayor of Gravesham
26/1/93	MR. & MRS TILTMAN parents of Victim
27/1/93	D/C/Supt. BLACKBURN D/SUPT BIDDIS.
29/1/93	Mayor of Swanscombe & Greenhythe Councillor Crow. D. ASHSMITH
29/1/93	A.C.C. AYLING Supt LOFTHOUSE / C/Insp Carlisle.
1/2/93	ACC HERMITAGE Supt CHATTON
2/2/93	D/C/Supt HIRST & team from Surrey. Review team
6/2/93	D/C/SUPT BLACKBURN
6/2/93	TINA CROCKFORD – Victim Support.

707

Visitor log for the incident room showing attendance among others by Chief Constable Paul Condon and Diane Ash-Smith (22 and 29 January 1993 respectively) (*Chapter 9*).

CHAPTER 9

Events Within Kent

As the calamitous events continued to unfold in south east London and Wimbledon, it barely touched the consciousness of the population of Greenhithe, until the night of the 18 January 1993 when Claire Tiltman, an innocent young woman, only just 16 years old was selected, targeted, attacked and murdered by an unknown knifeman. By the end of March the Kent investigating team were truly flummoxed. They were gradually eliminating all their possible suspects and the hoped-for forensics from the scene had proven completely negative.

A few apparently insignificant events associated with the investigation occurred which would attract interest and become most significant much later on. On 29 January 1993 the local mayor, Philip Crow and local labour councillor Mrs Diane Ash-Smith were invited to attend the incident room, which had by now been moved to a larger office at Northfleet Police Station to be brought up to date with the progress of the investigation. Considerable interest and concern had been provoked within the community who, believing there was a crazed murderer in their midst, needed reassurance.

A visitors' log at the incident room records them attending together, two days after the attendance of Claire's parents Linda and Cliff. Diane Ash-Smith knew the Tiltmans reasonably well. Both families were members of and frequent visitors to the British Legion Club in Greenhithe. Both were parents of a single child, and both encouraged their offspring to be involved at the British Legion. Diane's husband Aubrey was also a local councillor and on the committee at the club, so it followed that, although they could not be described as close friends and did not mix socially outside the environs of that club, they knew each other as more than just acquaintances.

Just what high priority the investigation had achieved in Kent can be gauged from the same document. On January 22, only three days after the murder, the incident room was visited by Kent's Chief Constable, Paul Condon who, within a short time in that same year, would become the Metropolitan Police Commissioner, carrying with him one high-profile unsolved murder, only to be saddled with another in the form of Rachel Nickell.

Mayor Crow and Councillor Ash-Smith were given the tour and the nuts and bolts of the investigation were explained, which hopefully gave them enough to carry back to their waiting community. Their visit was nothing out of the ordinary. Within the Greenhithe political scene the rivalries between opposing political factions were always put aside for the greater good and the leaders of both parties worked well together. Both asked the questions which had been highlighted by the community. Diane Ash-Smith was particularly interested in the unidentified car with the hazard warning lights flashing, which had been reported as being at the junction of London Road and Bean Road at or about the time of the murder. The visit to the incident room was a routine affair, with benefits to both the police and the community.

Mayor Crow and Mrs Ash-Smith together with her husband Aubrey also attended Claire's funeral. It was, as would be expected, a large affair, attended by a high proportion of the residents, showing their overwhelming sympathy to Linda and Cliff Tiltman. Accompanying Mr and Mrs Ash-Smith was their son Colin, who was at this time living at home with his parents in Milton Street, Swanscombe. He was currently working as a lifting equipment engineer at Ropequip in Erith. Colin was well known in the neighbourhood, mainly because he owned a striking white Ford Capri and loved to drive it around the local area. He was so attached to his 'wheels' he was hardly ever seen to walk anywhere, preferring to jump into his car even for the shortest of journeys. His social life revolved around the British Legion Club, which provided a convenient car park in which his distinctive car was often seen parked.

He was virtually unknown in the other local pubs at that time and did not travel much outside the environs of Greenhithe.

As previously described, Colin Ash-Smith was an only child born on 3 June 1968. His upbringing was within a loving and safe atmosphere. He hadn't shone academically at school and was known as a somewhat withdrawn and quiet child not given to mixing easily with other children. He developed a close friendship with another boy in primary school, Guy Hudson. They had met when they were placed in the same class in 1977 at Stone, the Brent primary school. The friendship continued after they were separated by their secondary school selection at the age of eleven. Guy went on to Dartford West Secondary and Colin to Downs Secondary. Despite this parting of the ways the two boys became ever closer, and Guy would spend weekends at Colin's house in Milton Street, Swanscombe. Guy went on holidays with the Ash-Smiths to Butlins Holiday Camp at Skegness and to Norfolk. Guy felt completely at home within the Ash-Smith household and was treated as another son.

In 1983, Guy moved away to stay with his grandmother in Dartford, but the friendship continued, and Colin would stay at Guy's grandmothers for weekends. Guy remembers Colin as being a perfectly normal adolescent boy. They shared an interest in listening to music and following football, both became Liverpool FC fans. In 1984 Colin was ready to enter the workplace and started with a firm in Dartford called Norvad, he also joined the Army Cadets at about this time. The friendship between Guy and Colin became less close for a while as both boys started new jobs. In May 1985, Guy struck up with a regular girlfriend who lived close to Colin and their friendship was rekindled. Later the relationship between Guy and his girlfriend ceased and in March 1986 Guy moved into the Ash-Smith family home in Milton Street where he stayed until moving out around March 1987. The two young men remained in close social contact throughout their moves and job changes. In June of 1988, Guy moved in with a woman in the nearby village of Darenth where he remained for the next five years during which time Colin Ash-Smith was a regular visitor, often staying over on Saturday nights with Guy's newly made family. Their main interest at this time was Gravesend United Football Club. Colin Ash-Smith became a fervent football fan, remotely supporting Liverpool FC and locally Gravesend United. He also qualified as a football referee although he found confrontations during matches difficult and his interest in refereeing waned.

After leaving secondary school Colin joined a youth training scheme which led to a job at a company called Norvad Ltd situated in Dartford. The company specialised in the manufacture of industrial strength lifting slings and he worked on the shopfloor. The work was steady and involved strictly enforced timekeeping, beginning at 7.30 am and finishing at 4.30 pm from Monday to Friday. He was described as quiet, but he mixed well with other workers. His work was slow but always to a high standard. He was a punctual timekeeper and rarely took time off work. In the mid 1980s Norvad Ltd was taken over by another company called Ropequip, a firm which dealt in the same business and took on most of the Norvad staff including Ash-Smith. The takeover resulted in a change of work location from Dartford to Swanley. Another town close to where Ash-Smith was living.

The workers at Ropequip all had knives with which they used to cut the ropes and strappings of the packages as they arrived in the factory. Colin's nickname at the factory was 'Phantom'. The reason for this was not as sinister as may appear, it was given because Colin was so quiet. He would seem to suddenly appear in a room without anyone noticing him enter. This was not seen as worrying but rather as a reflection of his shy and diffident manner. However, it was noted that Ash-Smith's knife was of the 'combat'-type and overly large. It was kept in a drawer on the premises.

Whilst Ash-Smith was working at Ropequip, Swanley, a young woman was attacked near a gravel pit in Swanscombe on 21 December 1988. The attacker had attempted to strangle her and used a knife and an air-pistol in the attack. The victim was badly injured and left unconscious at the scene. Swanscombe adjoins Greenhithe and is where Ash-Smith was living with his parents at this time, in Milton Street. The police released information to the public that part of a school tie had been left at the scene by the perpetrator. The tie was from Downs Secondary School, the same one Ash-Smith had attended four years previously.

It became a running joke with the workforce at Ropequip that the school tie belonged to the same school which Colin had attended. There was no other suggestion that Ash-Smith may have been responsible for the attack, and the police were not informed of this vague suspicion of his work colleagues. The sexually motivated offence was not solved and eventually was 'filed away' in the Kent Police records. Kent Police were to later find out how important this part of the jigsaw was when they came to investigate the knife attack on another young woman in Greenhithe seven years later, in October 1995.

As has been emphasised, Ash-Smith's other great hobby was his car. He had passed his driving test at the earliest opportunity and quickly graduated from driving his father's car to purchasing his own. He was driving a black Ford Capri up to 29 April 1992 when he took it to Motorpoint Quality Used Cars at Stafford Street Gillingham and part-exchanged it for another Ford Capri. This latest car, C404 CUL, was very distinctive, being white with a large 'whale tail' fitted to the rear section as a 'spoiler'. The car was also fitted with colour-coded skirting and pepper pot alloy wheels. It was not a runabout, it was a statement. At the time of the purchase Ash-Smith was still living with his parents at Milton Street, Swanscombe.

Several interesting points arise from the purchase of Colin Ash-Smith's renowned Ford Capri. His old car, the black Capri, was sent for a valet clean prior to resale. It was described as scruffy and unclean. During this cleaning a wooden handled knife was found under the driver's seat. The cleaner described the knife as having a shiny silver blade about 6" in length, which appeared to have been ground down. It had a wooden handle held in place with three brass rivets. The knife had the general appearance of a kitchen knife. The car cleaner, Tim Hunt, showed his find to the garage proprietor, Tim Kemp, who felt concerned enough to contact the police at Gillingham and inform them of what had been found. The police never attended the garage and the knife remained at the workshop being used for cutting up rags until it ended up in Tim Hunt's toolbox. There it remained until police renewed their interest in it and it was handed over to them on 26 October 1995 creating Exhibit TRH/1.

Colin Ash-Smith's social life remained centred around the British Legion Club in Greenhithe. He had little or no known contact with girls until this suddenly changed through his friend Guy Hudson, who had by now left his readymade family in Darenth and moved in with his new girlfriend Maria Murrell (who was to become his wife). Guy and Maria 'hatched a plan' for Ash-Smith to meet Maria's sister Stella. During Christmas 1991 they were introduced and hit it off immediately. Maria describes Ash-Smith as quiet, kind and helpful. The two couples shared the same flat for a while before Colin and Stella moved out to stay with Colin's parents in Milton Street, Swanscombe.

Whatever their domestic situations had changed into, the Hudsons and Stella and Colin Ash-Smith remained in close social contact. These meetings involved a branch out into the wider world for Colin. They would meet in The Plough pub in Northfleet on Friday evenings where the two couples would play pool, or Guy and Colin would watch football on the pub television. This newfound independence seemed to have a positive effect on Colin. He took a room at the beginning of 1995 at Beach Brow near the Pier Hotel in Greenhithe where he lived with Stella. Colin had also found himself redundant at Bridens, the final name change of his place of work, when the business closed down. He wasted no time and quickly took up a new occupation as a milkman.

Maria describes Colin as someone who was cool and calm and she never saw him lose his temper. He had the rather nerdish passion of computer games and was an avid fan of the *Star Trek* series. Although a regular at The Plough, Colin didn't drink alcohol or smoke. This made him stand out as it was a 'drinkers' pub. He was given, and took, graciously, some stick. He was known in The Plough as 'Ernie', after the Benny Hill milkman character of that name.

CHAPTER 10

The Downfall of Colin Ash-Smith

By early 1995 things were looking good for Colin Ash-Smith. He had regular employment in a job he enjoyed, and had set up home with a young woman with whom he shared a loving relationship. Then on Tuesday 17 October 1995 his world tumbled down about him. On that Tuesday, a young woman, Charlotte Barnard was at work at the Stone House Hospital in Dartford where she worked as a healthcare assistant. She finished work at 2.20 pm and met up with her friend Donna Banks, who also worked there and who gave her a lift in her car back to Charlotte's home in Greenhithe. The only deviation to her journey home was when Donna stopped at the Esso garage in London Road, Greenhithe, to top up her car with petrol. After the short stop Donna dropped Charlotte off at her house at 2.40 pm.

Charlotte greeted her grandmother, with whom she lived, and settled down before calling her friend, Louise Greenslade, to arrange a meeting at the Pier Hotel public house at 5 pm for a drink and a chat. The Pier Hotel is on the waterfront in the old part of Greenhithe and affords views over the River Thames. After making the arrangement to meet Louise she remained indoors.

At 4.45 pm, Charlotte telephoned for a cab from a local firm called Associated Taxis and it duly arrived at 4.55 pm to take her the distance of approximately one mile to the Pier Hotel. Charlotte was wearing a burgundy-coloured, thick, cotton, knee-length dress with a matching jacket of the same colour, black tights and black shoes with a one and half inch heel. Her hair was tied up in a ponytail. The cab took the direct route to the hotel and Charlotte went straight into the pub as she needed change from the bar to pay for the cab. Once the cabbie had been paid, she returned to the Pier Hotel where her friend Louise was waiting. They took up a place in the lounge side of the bar. Charlotte was familiar with the pub and had met Louise there a few times in the past at about the same time of day. She had also visited this same cosy venue with her boyfriend and others, so she knew it well and felt comfortable there.

The pub wasn't very busy and was hosting what Charlotte described as two or three locals standing at the bar whom she knew by sight, but not by name. The two women sipped their ciders and chatted as the pub gradually filled with more customers, none of whom Charlotte recognised to speak to. At 6.45 pm Charlotte and Louise decided to call it a day. As it was mid October, by this time of the evening it was already getting dark outside, and Charlotte decided to call for a cab. She thought of using the public telephone in the public bar but, by this time, the bar area was quite crowded and noisy, so she decided to walk to Greenhithe Railway Station (a distance of about a quarter of a mile) and telephone for a taxi from the call box by the steps to the station.[5]

It was a fine night, becoming dark and the streetlights were already on. She said goodbye to Louise who was intending to walk straight up the hill towards her boyfriend's house. Charlotte walked along High Street which is parallel to the river and left into Station Road. Walking in the kind weather, Charlotte felt unconcerned, being in familiar surroundings as she made her way to Greenhithe Railway Station. There were no other users of the footway in evidence as she made her way. The story of the unsolved murder of Claire Tiltman was a fading memory to the inhabitants of Greenhithe.

Station Road in 1995 was also different from how it is today. Where there is now a large roundabout which services the rebuilt railway station and dual carriageway towards Dartford, it was in 1995 a straightforward junction. The modern houses on the Dartford side of the road were yet to be built. The road at this time had a much more rural feel to it. At the entrance to Eagles Road the first of the new houses had already been built and were only recently occupied. Charlotte walked past these new houses on her left and became aware of a man walking towards her on

5. Greenhithe station has since been re-built. The steps remain although they are blocked off to the general public. There is a new entranceway and the public telephone has been removed.

the same side of the road. The man was dressed in dark clothing and had distinctive fair, almost yellow hair and a beard of a similar colour. When she was about ten feet away from him the man suddenly stopped, swore and bent down as if he'd dropped something. Charlotte carried on walking until, as she drew level with him, the man stood up and with his left hand put a knife to her throat. He moved round to the side of her and she felt the blade of the knife draw blood. He put his right arm around her, and terrified she felt as if she was going to faint. She managed to say, 'What do you want?' He replied in a quiet voice, 'Be quiet and shut up.'

Charlotte started to scream and he responded by dragging her across the road to a factory entranceway which was barred by gates. The gates were secured and would not open. As Charlotte continued to scream, she was stabbed repeatedly on the top half of her body. She put her hands up to defend herself and continued to scream as her attacker carried on stabbing her. She fell to the ground onto her back with her face towards the gates. By this time, she was petrified and convinced she was going to die.

Charlotte's injuries consisted of eight wounds to her back between her shoulder blades, one to her right rear side, and five to her right hand. Although the infliction of these wounds was terrifying, none were life threatening.

As suddenly as the attack happened, it stopped, and she heard the sound of her attacker's feet thudding on the pathway as he ran off in the direction of the railway station. Too terrified to move, she remained still, fearful in case the man should return. After she calculated the attacker would not do so, she rose to her feet and staggered towards one of the nearby houses. As she stumbled towards safety a female motorist driving from the direction of the Pier Hotel stopped and gave her assistance. By this time other people had responded to her screams for help and she was taken into a nearby house from where the ambulance and the police were called. Charlotte was taken to West Hill Hospital in Dartford where, upon examination, all of the wounds required stitching. But none were life-threatening. She was examined by Dr Bashistha Biswas who commented, 'All wounds superficial, just fat deep.'

Charlotte described her attacker as a white male of about 5' 8" in height of 'tubby' build. He had distinctive yellow hair cut short but with the appearance of having grown out, slightly wavy and untidy. He had a fair complexion and sported a stubbly beard the same colour as his hair. He was wearing dark-coloured tracksuit bottoms and a dark, sweatshirt-type, top and she believed he was wearing shoes. The man was aged between 28 and 32 years of age. The description was a good one. It belonged to Colin Ash-Smith. Charlotte was able to describe the knife as having a smooth 4" to 5" blade which was quite narrow and had a thick, substantial handle.

Unknown to Charlotte, her attacker, Ash-Smith, ran off towards the railway bridge where he had parked his white Ford Capri just 100 yards away. He drove off directly to his home which he shared with Stella at Beach Brow, Ingress Park, Greenhithe, near the Pier Hotel. Stella stated that on arrival Colin didn't seem in any way disturbed or out of the ordinary. She believed he had spent the day at Ruislip, north London, where he was booked in for a day's course in preparation to becoming a milkman after his redundancy from the engineering company, Norvad/Bridens at Erith. He started work almost immediately with Express Dairies and had begun a milk round which covered Farningham, South Darenth and Hextable, an area which was familiar and local to him.

Colin had attended the day book-keeping course at Ruislip. There had been a little mix up after he had left Stella in Greenhithe in the morning, driving off in his white Ford Capri. He hadn't gone far when he realised he'd forgotten his map with directions to the address in Ruislip. He stopped off at his parent's house at Stone (they had moved from Milton Street some nine months earlier in February 1995) between 7 and 7.30 am. He had his own key and let himself in, shouting up the stairs to his father Aubrey, asking if he could use the telephone. He telephoned Stella and then returned the short distance back to his own flat to collect his map before driving off to Ruislip.

After attending the course which finished at 2 pm Colin drove back to Greenhithe. However, he did not drive directly home to Beach Brow but instead to Stone to visit his parents, arriving between 4 and 4.30 pm. He chatted with his father whilst eating bread pudding in the living-room. Aubrey Ash-Smith describes his son's behaviour on the evening as completely normal. At about 6.15 pm Colin left his parents' house to 'Pick up Stella.' This he never did, instead he drove away in his Ford Capri and at some stage between his parent's house and his own flat decided to park his car in Station Road near the railway station. From there he walked the few yards to where he randomly and callously attacked Charlotte Barnard. A young woman who he did not know and with whom he had had no previous contact.

A witness, Gary King, lived opposite to where the attack happened in Station Road. He described how at 7.15 pm he was in his bedroom and heard screams coming from the direction of the road. The screams sounded desperate, so he opened his window to gain a better view. As he looked out, the screaming stopped and he saw a male walking swiftly along the opposite side of the road where at that time there was no pavement towards the direction of the railway station. He had a good uninterrupted view of the man describing him as aged in his late teens to early twenties, blond hair wearing a black bomber jacket. As the man strode off, he appeared to drop something. Gary King heard a distinctive metallic sound as the object hit the road. The man bent down to pick up whatever it was he had dropped. King informed the police of what he had seen and on 11 November 1995 he attended a formal identity parade at Chatham Police Station where he identified the man he had seen from his window as Colin Ash-Smith.

Paul Ettinger was in the front room of his house which also overlooked the spot where Charlotte had been attacked. His computer game was interrupted by his sister Catherine rushing into the room saying she had heard distressed screams from just outside. She later described it as one long scream followed by short outbursts as if the person screaming could not get enough air. To say that Colin Ash-Smith's behaviour was unusual in the wake of his attack on Charlotte would be an understatement to put it mildly, especially in the context of just how outwardly 'normal' he would appear. This ability to act as if nothing had happened was to trip him up when he later denied murdering Claire Tiltman. After he was seen by Paul Ettinger it would appear he drove straight home to Stella at Ingress Park, Greenhithe. A journey by motor vehicle of less than five minutes.

Stella had arrived home at 6.30 pm after being given a lift by a work colleague and after Colin had unexpectedly failed to pick her up. Between 7.15 pm and 7.30 pm (Stella cannot be sure of the exact time) she heard the key in the front door. She went to greet Colin and noticed he was still in the same clothes he had worn when he had left for work that morning. Everything appeared calm as Colin and Stella embraced by the door. She asked him if they were still going to The Plough that evening and he replied, 'Yeah. OK. Shall I get changed?' He started to look for other clothes to change into, then didn't bother and stayed in what he was wearing, a white t-shirt with a Liverpool motif, black army-style 'combat' trousers and black shoes. So dressed he left with Stella to drive to The Plough. They walked from their flat to where Colin's white Capri was parked near the Pier Hotel public house and then drove to The Plough in Northfleet.

Stella and Colin arrived at The Plough in Stonebridge Road, Northfleet at 7.25 pm. They were well-known customers, both known to the landlady Penelope Kirby. Penelope knew Stella rather better and Colin only by his first name, or because of his current occupation by his nickname Ernie. She described Stella as a warm, kind person with an outgoing personality. Conversely, Colin was quiet and reserved and difficult to talk to. They had been regulars at The Plough since early 1993 when Penelope and her partner had taken over there. She knew that the reason for Stella and Colin being in the pub that evening was because they were scheduled to play in a pool match, an event which did not take place as the other team failed to show up. Colin and Stella played pool together until the arrival of Stella's sister Maria and her husband Guy Hudson, another pair of regulars at the pub.

Penelope joined Stella and Maria in the public bar where they played darts together. Guy and Colin went through to the saloon bar to watch a game of football on the TV. Penelope did not notice anything out of the ordinary. Colin and Stella seemed very affectionate towards each other, especially Stella who pecked Colin on the cheek several times and was if anything even warmer and friendlier towards him than usual.

Colin drank his coca cola and some time, shortly after 10 pm, he and Stella left the pub. Although Penelope didn't see them drive away, she assumed they were in Colin's white Capri because he always, without fail, drove to the pub in it.

The time they departed from The Plough was confirmed by Monique Lavers who was a near neighbour of Ash-Smith and, although she did not know him by name, knew that he and Stella were lodgers at Beach Brow. On the evening of 17 October 1995 Monique was in her bedroom, sitting on her windowsill taking a telephone call from her boyfriend, when she saw Ash-Smith and Stella walking from the direction of the High Street towards Beach Brow. They passed within ten yards of her and she recognised them instantly. She could only estimate the time as between 9.45 pm and 10.15 pm. The timing at this point is not critical but it establishes the fact Stella and Colin returned directly home from The Plough.

Having driven directly back to Ingress Park, Stella and Colin went straight indoors. They didn't delay but went straight up to bed. At no time did Stella notice anything which made her suspicious about Colin's behaviour. This shows remarkable icy, self-control on behalf of Ash-Smith who had viciously attacked Charlotte Barnard less than three hours before. Meanwhile the police were busy at the scene of the attack on Charlotte. They were casting about for witnesses.

Geoffrey Juniper had been drinking in the Pier Hotel pub where he was a regular. On this particular evening he informed police he was imbibing non-alcoholic soda. At 7 pm he left the Pier Hotel to drive home in his red Volkswagen Golf which was parked outside that pub and drove off along the High Street turning left into Station Road. Although already dark it was a clear evening, and the lamplights gave good visibility along the roadside.

In Station Road he passed the junction to Eagles Road on his left. When he had driven a further 120 yards, he saw the figure of a male walking toward him on the railway station side of the road. He described the man as white, aged about 25 years, of average build and about 5' 8" tall. He had fair to ginger hair pushed back at the front and just over his collar at the back. He also had a beard which matched his hair colour. He was wearing a waist-length, front-zipped dark bomber-style jacket, dark trousers and dark shoes. As Juniper drove past within ten feet of the man, he recognised him as someone he'd seen nearby and lived in the vicinity of the Pier Hotel. As far as he was aware the man didn't use the Pier Hotel pub, but he knew he was the owner of a white Ford Capri which was often parked near to that pub. Although he did not know the man by name, he was able to remember which house he lived in on the Ingress Estate. He drove on until he saw by the railway bridge the same Ford Capri with its distinctive spoiler at the rear. The car was facing away from Greenhithe towards the London Road. There was nobody in the vehicle, but it did not appear to have been left in its current position for any period because the windows were clear of any misting. The vehicle appeared to have no-one in it. Without giving it too much thought Juniper carried on driving home. He was not to know that in a matter of moments Colin Ash-Smith was to attack and stab Charlotte Barnard.

Juniper arrived home at 7.10 pm where he stayed until 8.45 pm. Just before this time his sister-in-law had called in to drop off something and she told him of the stabbing of a young woman earlier in Greenhithe. The news concerned him so much he drove back to the Pier Hotel where he spoke to the resident chef and the barman who told him the police had been in the pub asking for any information. He made the decision to contact the police immediately and to pass on what he had seen earlier. He made a written statement to police that same evening at 11.45 pm not concluding it until 1 am.

James Spring visited the Pier Hotel at 6.55 pm on Tuesday October 17. He had just been to see his brother Ray who lived in Ingress Park. Coincidentally, Ray lived next door to where Colin Ash-Smith resided with Stella. He had seen Ash-Smith on a number of occasions and although he knew him by sight had never spoken to him as Ash-Smith did not appear to want to engage in chit chat. Spring had also noted that Ash-Smith owned and drove a white Ford Capri with a distinctive whale tail spoiler. He took particular notice as he was the owner of a vehicle windscreen and body replacement company and had dealt with vehicles on a daily basis for many years. Whilst visiting his brother he did not see the Capri parked in any of the usual places. He returned to his Ford Escort van and, in order to do so passed the front entrance of the Pier Hotel, then decided to go in. He had one pint of lager top and then left as he had to pick up his son in Dartford at 7.10 pm. Leaving the Pier Hotel at 7.05 pm, he then drove up The Avenue and turned right into Eagles Road and on to the end. At the junction with Station Road he turned left towards Greenhithe Railway Station. As he turned into Station Road he saw the figure of a young woman walking alone towards the railway station. From his description and the timing this could only have been Charlotte Barnard. He didn't see any other person in the area and only one car, a white Ford Capri which was parked very close to the railway bridge facing the A226. There was no-one sitting in or near the vehicle that he could see but he recognised the car immediately as the one which belonged to Colin Ash-Smith.

Stella and Colin were in bed when, at 12.30 am, the doorbell rang accompanied by a loud knocking on the door. Stella answered and was greeted by plainclothes police officers who asked to speak to Colin. The police then arrested Colin for the attack on Charlotte and took him with them to Dartford Police Station. Meanwhile other officers conducted a search of the Beach Brow property and took away Colin's Ford Capri.

Over the next few days and weeks police interviewed Stella on several occasions. She was shown a 1988 diary entitled 'My fantasies with Debbie Jarvis 2'. This diary had been found in the Beach Brow flat taped to the underside of a table. It contained a graphic account of Ash-Smith's attack on Beverley Godfrey back in December 1988.

The diary listed four 'Assault Plans' only one of which was established by the evidence to be real (that on Beverley). The other three were 'failures' and didn't actually happen. He had marked up the attack on Beverley Godfrey in December 1988 as 'MY MASTERPIECE'. Of the four attacks listed by Ash-Smith only the one on Beverley Godfrey can be confirmed as actually having happened. No mention was made anywhere within the diary or in any other of Ash-Smith's seized documents of an attack in 1993 on Claire Tiltman. An oversight of Ash-Smith which is beyond curious if he had, as the Kent investigators claimed, murdered her with apparent impunity and felt he was beyond suspicion. A strange anomaly in the Ash-Smith diary is that he refers to the attack on Beverley Godfrey as being in December 1989 when it was in December 1988. It does make one wonder when he wrote up the diary.

Stella had no knowledge of the document. She was also shown the photograph of a flick knife which she failed to recognise. This knife had been found outside their flat where it had been thrown by Ash-Smith after the police had come to call and just prior to his arrest. Stella had already told police she was aware of Colin owning a flick knife which he kept variously in his car or at home and she had seen Colin with a similar knife a few days prior to the Barnard attack. She was also shown one of her own old calendars which referred to 18 January 1993 (the date of the Tiltman murder). Stella had written the words 'Music Course' against that date. She was certainly with Colin in early 1993 but could not remember the day specifically, although she remembered attending a course for her work at about that time.

There is no doubt that Stella was heavily under the influence of Colin Ash-Smith. Their relationship was dominated by him, and he could be very controlling towards her, forbidding her to meet with friends or interact socially without his approval. This said, Stella was never, ever subjected to physical violence. On the contrary, Ash-Smith would often behave in a very affectionate manner. However, his moods could change very quickly. In her naïvety, Stella put his oppressive moments down to over-protectiveness. At the time of Claire's murder Stella and Colin were seeing each other but Stella was still living at her parents' house and Colin was living in Milton Street with his parents. Stella had only met Claire Tiltman in passing at the British Legion Club and had not spoken to her. The relationship between Stella and Colin provides a fascinating view into his character. On the surface a fairly typical, growing, romantic entanglement but when looked at in more detail, and in the light of Colin's known offences, a rather strange liaison.

Stella seems to have had no knowledge of Colin's violent side, or his fantasies. In fact, their own sexual relationship depended more on her instigation than his. They lived together for a while at Colin's family home in Swanscombe but, whilst there, did not share the same bedroom. This was not out of any prudish directive from Colin's parents but a matter of Colin's own choice. Colin informed Stella that he wanted his privacy, any sexual relations were conducted in her room. Stella, years later, after she had been exposed to a wider view of life's experiences, would explain that Colin did have problems with erectile dysfunction, something which, at the time she did not fully understand.

In a statement made by Stella, much later in October 2013, when she knew she was suffering from terminal cancer, she made a frank revelation to police of her relationship with Ash-Smith. She explained in-depth how not only was she dominated by Colin but in turn she believed Colin was dominated by his friend, her brother-in-law, Guy Hudson. She described Colin as 'a dogsbody' for Guy, someone for whom he would unquestioningly run errands. She describes Hudson as Colin's long-term and only friend.

At the time of Claire's murder she remembered how Colin told her about it. He said he was really upset because he'd known Claire socially. He also told her he found it too difficult to talk about. After Claire's murder the evening telephone conversations between the couple, which had often lasted over an hour, ceased and Colin withdrew into himself. She tried to engage with him, but he became sullen and aggressive. He forbade her from attending Claire's memorial service with him. She barely saw him for two weeks after Claire's death. This odd behaviour was later seen as tantamount to an admission of guilt. Read into it what you will.

After a few weeks Colin became affectionate again and it was then that Stella moved in with him at his parents' house in Milton Street. They didn't live there for very long before they found the flat at Beach Brow on the Ingress Estate near the Pier Hotel in Greenhithe. Once installed in Beach Brow and away from Guy's and Colin's parents' influence, their relationship improved, although they remained in fairly close contact with Guy and Maria and the Ash-Smiths. The improvement in their relationship continued to settle and strengthen but Colin was still very controlling. He told Stella that, if she ever got pregnant, he would know she was having an affair because it couldn't be his. It was at about this time mobile phones were becoming widespread. Colin would not allow her to have one as he didn't want her 'talking to other people'. He could be nasty and impatient towards her but to everyone else he was very placid.

Just before Colin was arrested, the couple were in fact looking around to buy a house together and had become engaged to be married. Though Colin's somewhat odd behaviour continued. One of the signs of his control over Stella was his insistence that she got up early in the morning, the same time as him, before he started his milk round. After Colin's arrest Stella made her way to Aubrey and Diane's house where she banged on their door to awaken them. She informed them about it but was unsure of the details. Aubrey drove Stella and Diane back to Beach Brow where they found police were still at the scene and were told the reason for his arrest and that he'd been taken to Dartford Police Station.

For reasons which even Stella cannot explain, once she found out the full reason for Colin's arrest she wasn't at all shocked and it did not come as a major surprise to her. She returned to the Ash-Smith house with Diane and Aubrey. Stella moved in with them and over the next few days they tried to come to terms with what Colin had been arrested for. The Ash-Smiths could not believe their only son could have committed such a heinous offence. Stella was placed under enormous pressure from all angles, and it is not surprising that initially she turned to the Ash-Smith family for support. In her police interview she tried to explain the family dynamics of the Ash-Smith household. She had a closer view than anyone else and her views are relevant as it may have coloured the attitude of the police investigators towards the senior Ash-Smiths. Almost immediately Stella regretted making her statement to police and became very suspicious of the police investigation. This resulted in her contacting a solicitor who sent a letter on the 3 November 1995 to the investigating team retracting her witness statement and saying she was in a state of shock at the time of making it and some of the things she said may not actually be true.

Just before Colin's arrest there had been a domestic row in the family over a brief affair Diane had been having. One of these heated arguments led to revelations from Aubrey, in the presence of Colin, that Diane had been raped when she was very young and had given birth to a baby girl. This came as a great shock to Colin and he insisted on meeting his older half sister. At about the same time, Diane had been made Mayor of Greenhithe. Aubrey was also involved in politics and a councillor. Stella claimed she felt there was some underlying jealousy between Aubrey and Diane because Diane had been nominated ahead of him.

The conversations in the Ash-Smith's house were regular and intense. Stella remembers being told by Diane how she had found an old, ripped school tie of Colin's under his pillow in his bedroom at Milton Street. Diane even went to the trouble of repairing it by stitching it back together not realising the significance of it's evidential value in the attack on Beverley Godfrey. Stella made the claim about Diane's knowledge of the tie in a statement made in 2013 and in her tape-recorded interviews with DC Jobes, also in 2013. It must be mentioned that she made no reference to it in her statements made after Colin's arrest in 1995.

Stella could also remember that the question surrounding the murder of Claire was a topic that was never broached, and the possibility of Colin's involvement was never mentioned. She stayed at the Ash-Smith's house during Colin's trial for the attacks on Charlotte and Beverley and up until the date she actually married Colin in prison in 1997. The marriage, according to Stella, was after an ultimatum from the Ash-Smiths to either marry Colin or leave the house. This was given by Colin supported by his parents on one of the prison visits. The visits to Colin in prison were a stressful experience for Stella, especially as she was always discouraged by the Ash-Smiths from ever visiting him on her own. She was always accompanied by Aubrey or Diane or both and they would always dominate the conversation and the visit. During one particularly stressful visit, Stella became frustrated at Aubrey preventing her from touching Colin, culminating in Aubrey tapping her on the back of her head, when she lost control and turned on him and punched him. During the few times she was able to get a word in, she asked Colin directly if he had committed the two crimes he had been arrested for. Although reluctant to talk about them Colin did reply, 'Yes I did do that stuff' (meaning the attacks on Charlotte and Beverley). She only asked him once about Claire to which he replied, 'No, I didn't do it.'

Less than a month after her marriage to Colin in 1997 Stella started a new job and moved out of the Ash-Smith household. She also used the move to start divorce proceedings which Colin contested and it wasn't for another two years before the divorce was finalised. At this time Stella detached herself completely from the Ash-Smith family. During this period of her life she was variously under the influence of those around her and it wasn't until she finally managed to break free and make her own life, re-marrying and starting her own family, that she was able to analyse what had happened more dispassionately. It must be said however that, looking back, Stella did come to the conclusion that Ash-Smith was responsible for the murder of Claire Tiltman. In her own words given in a police interview on 10 October 2013 she said, 'I think he saw an opportunity of a young girl on her own, stopped, got a bit of a shock when he realised it was someone he knew, and felt that he just had to kill her. I think he's done it.' She continued, 'Because of everything else he's done. He's done all this other stuff, its exactly the same sort of place, the same sort of thing he's done before. Why react like that over someone he didn't seem to know? When I saw her [Claire] he just grunted "Hello".'

There was a pause and then she continued, 'I remember what happened with Claire, because he changed so dramatically. That sort of thing you remember.' It is interesting to note that at the end of the interview the interviewing officer told Stella the re-investigation was in its early stages and although Ash-Smith was a suspect for the murder of Claire there was no evidence to charge him at that time.

Stella it seems showed some concern about Colin's possible release from custody. At this time in 2013, he had served 17 years of his life sentence for the attacks on Beverley and Charlotte. Stella was still concerned he might try and get back into her life and (with the added worry she had that he may have murdered Claire) might do her some serious harm. Her belief and its inclusion in her consequent statement that Ash-Smith had murdered Claire Tiltman, although based on some logic, carried no weight and was I believe borne more out of fear than knowledge. Stella was terminally ill when she made this statement to police and even though she was hopeful of having another ten years of life and stated her willingness to give evidence at any future trial, she was to pass away within the year on 11 July 2014 a few months before the looming trial.

CHAPTER 11

Post-arrest Back in 1995

Colin Ash-Smith was taken in custody to Dartford Police Station where the circumstances of his arrest on suspicion of the attack on Charlotte Barnard were explained to the custody sergeant who authorised his detention. Word was getting around of his arrest and at about 3 am on the Wednesday morning of 18 October 1995 Ash-Smith's friend, Guy Hudson turned up at the police station in Dartford. He became abusive towards the female officer on duty, WPC Turner. Hudson ranted about how the police had arrested his 'best mate' for the stabbing at Greenhithe. His rant became more abusive as he shouted that the police 'had the wrong man'. He demanded to see the officer in charge saying, 'If you don't get the main man down here now, I'm going to go out and kill some mother fucking copper now.' Hudson was demonstrating with somewhat excessive zeal in getting his point across. Sgt Cooper came down to the front desk and after giving Hudson 'advice' he left the police station. This departure was short lived as he returned to the front desk a few minutes later where he continued with his threats and abuse until he was eventually arrested for disorderly behaviour and placed in the cells.

Meanwhile in another part of the police station an incident room was being set up for the investigation into Charlotte's stabbing. D Supt Nick Biddiss was appointed to head the enquiry. Meanwhile senior SOCO, Michael House was at the Beach Brow flat assisting with the post-offence search. Whilst there he entered into a conversation with another SOCO, Andrew Broomham. The two discussed the case and Broomham mentioned that when he was searching Ash-Smith's Ford Capri, in the boot amongst other things he had found part of an old school tie. Michael House's ears immediately pricked up. He had been the SOCO at the investigation of the attempted murder of Beverley Godfrey back in December 1988. During that attack a school tie had been used in an attempt to strangle her. The tie had split in two foiling the attempt. One half of the tie had been left at the scene and the other had never been recovered.

SOCO Broomham was immediately despatched to recover the tie and preserve it for examination against the other piece of the tie, which was still in police possession as an outstanding exhibit (SJH/1) from the Godfrey assault. On 20 October, Broomham attended Gravesend Police Station where, in the secure property section, he recovered the part of the school tie recovered from the Godfrey scene. On the same day he took the two parts (now labelled Exhibits SJH/1 and AB/29) to the forensic laboratory at Aldermaston. After a scientific examination it came as no surprise to Broomham that the two pieces of tie were a mechanical fit and were without doubt two parts of the same item.

It later transpired that the tie found in the boot of the Capri was the one allegedly mended by Diane Ash-Smith. What it was doing in the boot of Colin Ash-Smith's car can only be explained by Ash-Smith. Perhaps he was carrying it around as a trophy of his past misdeed. An offence, which by now, seven years later, he must have reasoned he was in the clear for. This revelation and brilliant piece of detective work now linked Ash-Smith to two attempted murders of young women who were strangers to the assailant and were attacked seemingly at random in public places, in darkness, and in areas local to him.

How fortunate that SOCO Michael House was involved in the 1988 investigation and was alive to the possibility of a link. The piece of school tie had been popped into a property bag of 'Sundry Items' with the rest of the detritus in Ash-Smith's car. Items which were on first assessment deemed 'not to be relevant to the offence being investigated'. Now the police could evidentially link Ash-Smith to two attacks. As surely as night follows day, he must be responsible for the Claire Tiltman attack? It too was committed in the hours of darkness on a lone female, in a public place, all within the area near to where the assailant lived, using a knife. The police view was (not unnaturally) that Ash-Smith must be responsible for Claire's murder.

It is worth bearing in mind at this point that during the investigation into the murder of Rachel Nickell the psychological profiler Paul Britton famously declared,

> 'I can only say that the probability of there being two people on Wimbledon Common that morning who suffered from the same extreme and violence-oriented sexual deviation is incredibly small.'[6]

This statement was made after his psychological profile pertaining to the Wimbledon offence had been completed and which led to the arrest of Colin Stagg. The profile seemed to affirm the probability of Stagg being Rachel's murderer. Stagg was now believed by many, including the national press and politicians, to be a psychopathic killer. This view gave rise to the theory of there being an infinitesimal chance of there being another such disturbed person performing in the same small location at the same time.

Paul Britton's assumption was absolutely correct, there was only one psychopath on Wimbledon Common on the day of Rachel's murder, but it wasn't Colin Stagg. The investigating team had fallen into the trap of 'confirmation bias'. Britton's words were music to the police investigators' ears. The Kent investigators did consider using the services of Britton and he was contacted by them. The Operation Artist review of 2003 mentions a profile completed by him for them. To quote Para 9, 'The above relates to a profile prepared by Paul Britton, Clinical psychologist'. The profile was intended to be used 'in house' and not for circulation. It would be extremely interesting to have had a psychological profile to compare with those made in the Green Chain, Nickell and Bisset cases.

Colin Ash-Smith was subjected to interview beginning on the evening of the 18 October 1995. At first, he stonewalled and gave the stock reply 'No comment' on his solicitor's advice and to all questions. A 'No comment' interview is a time-honoured technique and is perfectly

6. Paul Britton, *The Jigsaw Man*, p. 414.

acceptable under the rules of the Police and Criminal Evidence Act 1984. Conversely, it does have the adverse effect of heightening the suspicions of the interviewing officers. In this particular incident the evidence kept filtering through to the incident room. It wasn't long before information of the torn school tie found in Ash-Smith's car being matched to the part of the tie used in the Beverley Godfrey attack was available to the investigators.

As noted in *Chapter 10*, further searches of addresses to which Ash-Smith had access revealed a diary containing explicit sexual fantasies, which included knife attacks on women. A blue jacket recovered from his Beach Brow address had what appeared to be blood staining on the right cuff and inside a pocket. Tests revealed these to be the blood of Charlotte Barnard. A police team searched the garden adjacent to the Beach Brow address on October 19 and at 12.03 pm PC 8423 Marshall found, underneath a patch of long grass, a green handled flick knife. It was lying in the open position with the blade showing. This find was logged as Exhibit GDM/1.

A more productive series of interviews took place at Dartford Police Station commencing on 10 November 1995. At first Ash-Smith gave up a few personal details such as the reason why he had given up drinking alcohol (he'd become so drunk on his nineteenth birthday he was incapable of standing and he hadn't taken alcohol since). It was put to him he was responsible for other attacks in the area especially referring to a young woman attacked at Greenhithe Railway Station in 1994. This he denied. In a further interview conducted the next day, it was put to him that both Geoffrey Juniper and James Spring had identified him as the man seen near the Charlotte Barnard attack. He gave a 'No comment' answer to this.

On 20 November 1995 he was rearrested on suspicion of the murder of Claire Tiltman and interviewed at 12 pm. During this interview he told the interviewing officers the only thing he knew about Claire's murder was what he had read in the newspapers. He remembered giving a witness statement to police at the time of the murder in which he mentioned seeing a male whom he could not identify in London Road whilst he was driving his car at about 6.30 pm. He said he did know

Claire and had played pool with her at the British Legion Club. He had been working at Bridon Ropes in Erith on the day of the murder, the 18 January 1993, and got home to his parents' address in Milton Street, Swanscombe at his usual time of 4.30 pm. At 5.30 pm his mother Diane announced she was going to deliver some paperwork to do with council business to a constituent Mr Wells in Eynsford Road and Colin volunteered to drive her there. He drove his mother in his white Ford Capri going via Knockhall Chase. He remained in his car whilst Diane walked up the short drive to deliver the paperwork. Colin thought he could remember his mother talking at the doorway for four or five minutes, always within sight before returning to the car. This recollection, three years after the event, was not substantiated by his mother Diane who was sure she only delivered a letter and returned immediately to Colin's car. The relevance of the discrepancy I would suggest is unimportant.

They drove straight home without stopping, via Mounts Road turning left into Alkerden Lane. At no time on the return journey did he drive in London Road. The entire trip took less than half-an-hour. His father, Aubrey, was at home when they both arrived and confirmed this. Aubrey left the house at 7 pm to go to the British Legion Club to help host a bingo night, leaving his wife Diane in the house with Colin. Colin then remained indoors throughout the entire evening before retiring to bed. Diane was with him during all of this time. He told the interviewers he had attended Claire's funeral. He was now asked, 'Did you kill Claire?' to which he replied with an emphatic 'No.'

Police were left with a few inconsistencies to ponder over. Firstly, in his witness statement given shortly after the murder and long before he became a suspect he describes how, whilst he was with his mother in London Road at 6.30 pm, he saw an unknown person who he could not tell whether male or female. His father Aubrey stated he was home asleep when his wife and son returned and fixed the time by his wristwatch and the five clocks in the room at 6.05 pm. Diane Ash-Smith had no recollection of seeing the unidentified person in London Road but confirmed they were home and indoors by 6.05 pm. She also differed slightly in the route home given by Colin. As with Colin she was trying to recall events in detail that had happened three years previously.

The police could take a balanced view. It was almost three years since the murder of Claire and memories could understandably be fuzzy. Although Colin's original statement was almost contemporaneous, Mr and Mrs Ash-Smith were adamant they were both indoors at 6.05 pm with Colin at the time of the murder which was estimated to have been at 6.15 pm. Aubrey Ash-Smith then managed to completely discredit himself by attempting to destroy a knife belonging to his son by boiling it, damaging it and disposing of it. An offence for which he was charged and later sentenced to 12 months' imprisonment. Diane Ash-Smith by implication became enmeshed in this sorry attempt to pervert the course of justice.

The officer who arrested Diane Ash-Smith for this alleged attempt was D Sgt Peter Brisley. From this time onwards he also became involved in the unsolved murder of Claire Tiltman. Shortly after Colin was arrested for the attack on Charlotte Bernard, he conducted Colin's police interview for that offence. A few weeks later, Colin was further arrested on suspicion of murdering Claire. Lack of evidence meant that this allegation was soon dropped. D Sgt Brisley was regarded as highly knowledgeable about both Operation Zulu (the Godfrey case) and Operation Artist (the Tiltman case). Something remarked upon in the official Tiltman case review in 2003. It was naturally considered essential that he be included in the review team. However, by his retirement in 2009, the Tiltman murder remained unsolved (D Supt Biddiss who was in overall charge during this period retired a few years earlier).

Post-retirement, Peter Brisley was employed by Kent Police as a civilian investigator. One can see why someone with such resources to hand was allowed to 'stay on the case'. But to my mind and given the need to keep everything under constant review, it may have been wiser had the investigation been allowed to become less susceptible to any existing preconceptions. As elsewhere in this book, I do not seek to criticise the work of individuals, especially those so dedicated, experienced and professional. Rather, a system that does not routinely challenge such risks.

The remains of the knife were recovered but it was shown without doubt that it could not have been used in the Tiltman attack. However, the damage was done. The police investigators found it extremely difficult, if not impossible, to believe anything further from the Ash-Smith family.

It was put to Colin Ash-Smith that he had tried to mislead the police in 1993 by stating he had seen an unknown person near the murder scene, that he had made up an alibi and had in fact been in that part of London Road at the relevant time of 6.15 pm. He was asked, again point blank, if he had murdered Claire. Again, he gave an emphatic 'No.'

Ash-Smith was asked if his father Aubrey had made up the story of his returning home at 6.05 pm to give him a false alibi. He was told about Aubrey destroying evidence by disposing of the knife. Colin appeared surprised, responding that he had no answer as to why Aubrey would do such a thing because he had nothing to hide regarding the murder of Claire. Another explanation which might have been considered by the interrogators was that the reason Aubrey said Colin was in the house at 6.05 pm was because all of them were there, at home, and Colin *hadn't* killed Claire.

At this point in the interview an element of ill feeling crept into the proceedings and Colin Ash-Smith reverted to his safety mode of 'No comment.' The interview was going nowhere, that is, until the senior investigating officer, D Supt Biddiss entered the interview room and almost immediately probed Colin's story. The style was fairly gentle at first as Biddiss went over the same ground. Ash-Smith was at least responding to questions again and when Biddiss asked him if he had murdered Claire his reply was more expansive: 'I was 100% not there. A 100%. I am willing to take any test. I know I wasn't there.' He then readily admitted to the attack on Charlotte but would still only at this stage give 'No comment' as a reply to any questions about Beverley. Frustration had been building up and Colin's solicitor Robin Murray made strong objections to the interview style. As tempers frayed Murray declared to Biddiss that the interview was illegal and would not be allowed in evidence in court. It was an angry scene as the interview drew to a close.

Ash-Smith was then returned to his cell. It was during his time in the police cell that he wrote a note explaining his regrets over what had happened and then, using sheeting, attempted to commit suicide. The attempt was half-hearted and a doctor was summoned. There were no serious injuries and after seeing the doctor, who noted red marks on his neck, he was declared fit to continue the interview and Ash-Smith requested to speak to the police. At 7.12 pm his interview resumed with D Supt Biddiss.

It was during this interview that Ash-Smith made his confession to the attacks on Beverley in 1988 and Charlotte on 17 October 1995 (one month prior to the interview). He also gave helpful pointers to Biddiss by admitting the knife found outside his flat at Beach Brow was the one he had used in the attack on Charlotte, and the blue jacket taken from his flat with blood staining on the sleeve and pocket was the one he was wearing during that attack. He informed Biddiss that after the attack on Charlotte he went straight to his Ford Capri and drove directly home, taking a route along London Road and then down the hill towards the Pier Hotel and Beach Brow where he parked in the street.

Ash-Smith tried to explain why he had committed such appalling acts. He confessed to having fantasies about attacking women, but he was (with the exception of Beverley and Charlotte) able to pull himself out of it. He said, 'I don't know why I did it. It's like an impulse. Mostly I just snap out of it.' On the evening he had attacked Charlotte he had left his parents' house in Stone and stopped by the railway station to use the public telephone. He had been having fantasies about attacking a woman and the situation just presented itself.

The interview was moved on to encourage him to confess to the attack on Claire Tiltman. At first Ash-Smith was co-operative explaining the discrepancy in times between the witness statement he had provided shortly after Claire's murder in which he put himself in London Road at 6.30 pm and his later account of being home by 6.05 pm. He said he simply got the times wrong and when he later discussed it with his mother and father they pointed out they were definitely indoors by 6.05 pm. The interview again became frosty when it was put to Ash-Smith that the unidentified figure he had seen by the zebra crossing in London Road was fictitious and made up by him to give himself an alibi. The vague figure described did bear a slight resemblance to himself.

When asked again if he had murdered Claire Tiltman he replied, 'Out of all the interviews I've been in I haven't told one single lie. I can categorically say I had nothing to do with Claire's murder ... There is no way I am involved in a cover up.' As the interviewers became more insistent and the accusations of Ash-Smith's involvement in Claire's murder became more repetitive Ash-Smith reverted after the advice of his solicitor Robin Murray to the 'No comment' mode of response to all questions.

The police prepared their cases for trial. From one perspective they had had a good day. The man responsible for two sexually motivated attacks on women in the Greenhithe area had been arrested and had confessed to those crimes. On the other hand, the crime they were most keen to solve remained just out of their reach. What are the chances of a predatory sex offender operating in a small area over a number of years not being responsible for the murder of Claire Tiltman? It was the general view of officers of all ranks in the Kent Police that the chances of there being two dangerous, sexual predators operating on the same patch were negligible. They unhesitatingly took the giant leap. Having done so, it was only a series of small steps to the chosen suspect being the *only* suspect and all subsequent intelligence being filtered towards demonstrating his guilt.

The trial of Robert Napper had only just been concluded in September 1995 at the Central Criminal Court. On 10 October 1995, he was found guilty of the series of Green Chain Rapes in 1992. He was also found guilty of the manslaughter of Samantha and Jazmine Bisset in November 1993. This result caused barely a ripple in the national press as Napper took up residence at a facility for the criminally insane, Broadmoor. In any event Napper was definitely not linked to the Rachel Nickell murder as he was perceived to operate exclusively in a confined area of south east London, and the murder of Claire Tiltman was 'a Kent job', south east London was miles away ... Or only four stops down the line according to your perspective. Napper settled down to his quiet life in Broadmoor, accompanied by a collective sigh of relief from murder detectives and complete indifference from the Nickell and Tiltman murder teams.

categorically say I had nothing to do with it. [illegible] there is no way I am involved in a cover up.' As the interview [illegible] became more [illegible] on the accusations of Ashdown's involvement in Claire's murder, [illegible] Ashdown [illegible] the advice of his [illegible] Robin [illegible] to the 'No comment' mode of response to all questions.

The police prepared the[ir] case [illegible] from one perspective: that [illegible] the man responsible for the sexually motivated attacks on women in the [illegible] had been [illegible] and had [illegible] those [illegible] to the other [illegible] the crime they were meant to solve remained just out of their reach. What are the chances of a predatory [illegible] offender [illegible] in a small area over a number of years not being responsible for the murder of Claire Tiltman? It leaves the general view of officers of all ranks in the Kent Police that the chances of there being two dangerous sexual predators operating on the same patch were negligible; they unwittingly took the [illegible]. Having done so, it was only a series of small steps to the chosen suspect being the only suspect and all subsequent enquiries being directed towards demonstrating his guilt.

The [illegible] of Robert Napper had only just been concluded in September 1995 at the Central Criminal Court. On 30 October 1995 he was found guilty of the series of Green Chain Rapes in 1992. He was also found guilty of the manslaughter of Samantha and Jazmine Bisset in November 1993. This report caused hardly a ripple in the national press as Napper took up [illegible] indefinitely in Broadmoor. In any event, Napper was determined not to be linked to the Rachel Nickell murder as he was perceived to operate exclusively in [illegible] south east London, and the murder of Claire Tiltman was in Kent. South east London was miles away but [illegible] only four stops down the line [illegible]. In retrospective, Napper settled down to his quiet life in Broadmoor, accompanied by a collective sigh of relief from [illegible] detectives and complete indifference from the Nickell and Tiltman murder teams.

CHAPTER 12

A Gift from the Gods

'I never guess. It is a shocking habit, destructive to the logical faculty' — Sherlock Holmes courtesy of Arthur Conan Doyle, *The Sign of Four.*

An alternative title for this chapter might have been 'Guessing: How Reason Proceeds in the Absence of Facts'. When Colin Ash-Smith fell into the lap of the Kent Police in 1995 it didn't take them long to realise they had a serial sex offender living in and committing offences in the same locale as one of their most high-profile and unsolved murders of the past ten years. They had been investigating the murder of Claire Tiltman ever since her death on 18 January 1993. No breakthroughs had happened, and no firm suspect had come to the fore until Ash-Smith blundered into their field of vision when he attacked Charlotte Barnard in October 1995. Certainly, it is an accepted fact that during all the intervening time between Claire's death and Charlotte's attack, Ash-Smith had never once been considered a suspect. Throughout this period only one person had been treated as a viable suspect. A man with severe mental health issues called Peter Rivers.

On 24 January 1994 the Tiltman murder incident room at Northfleet Police Station was closed down. The SIO, D Supt Owen Taylor was obliged to scale down the inquiry and with a smaller team move to Gravesend Police Station. Taylor put a brave face on it, declaring, 'We will not ever give up the Claire file. It will stay open forever.'

The closure of an incident room is not unusual, even in high-profile investigations. Resources must be used as efficiently as possible and when an enquiry runs out of steam it is a natural consequence that precious resources are re-directed elsewhere. The files are stored and, with the main body of work almost instantly available via HOLMES, should any further information come into police possession it is a straightforward matter, not simple but straightforward, to reactivate computer records.

On 1 February 1994, the case received a boost after the mentally-disturbed Peter Rivers murdered his mother in a house they shared in Dartford and then took his own life. He left a note at the scene indicating he had a connection to the murder of Claire Tiltman and that because of his mother's knowledge of this he was driven to kill her. The scrawled, handwritten suicide note, which was heavily bloodied, contained one brief sentence, 'Mum was beginning to suspect me of killing Claire.' Hardly a resounding confession, but enough for the enquiry to examine the facts. The events were to achieve renewed prominence in the future trial of Ash-Smith for the murder of Claire (see *Chapter 17*). Serious consideration was given to the possibility of Rivers having killed Claire but, apart from his suicide note, which was not really a 'confession', absolutely nothing else was discovered to link Rivers to her in any capacity.

Ash-Smith, after he had attacked Charlotte in October 1995, was a far stronger suspect. He had admitted attacking two young women using a knife. The attacks were sexually motivated, the victims were chosen at random, and they were both within a very limited location. The attacker had a fascination with knives. He was careless as to whether he might be caught in the act. The crimes themselves could have easily resulted in one or both victims being fatally hurt. He had the capacity to revert to a 'normal' lifestyle to avoid suspicion after the event and showed no obvious signs of real remorse. He therefore must be responsible for murdering Claire, mustn't he? The logic is faultless and any investigator worth their salt would immediately be attracted to the idea that Ash-Smith had murdered Claire and should be treated as the number one suspect. This is the path the investigators now rightly took.

In the intervening two-and-a-half years since the murder, the original SIO, D Supt Taylor had fallen sick and been diagnosed with cancer. His position had been taken over by D Supt Biddiss, a very experienced CID officer. Owen Taylor was to die in 1997. He had built up a close relationship with Claire's parents, Linda and Cliff Tiltman. So embedded was he with the family that his name appears on the memorial to Claire which was placed at the entrance to the alleyway in London Road. The death of this dedicated and popular officer also left an indelible mark on the investigating team and on his successor. The murder of Claire Tiltman had to be solved.

There is nothing unusual or wrong in such a close attachment by an investigator to the bereaved's family. It is an intense atmosphere in the environs of a murder investigation, especially one as heartrendingly sad as the murder of an innocent child. Those of us who have been involved in such circumstances can only sympathise with the mixture of the same feelings the investigators would have had, feelings which cause an assault on the innermost private thoughts of those brought in to investigate a tragedy such as this. It is impossible to remain totally detached. However, despite our sympathies, it is imperative we retain a strong sense of impartiality. This is not to say adopt a callous attitude, but rather to remind all those on the investigating team to retain an open mind on all information which enters the system.

It is galling to watch the development of 'confirmation bias' and for this to take hold and sometimes dominate an investigation. I witnessed this syndrome at first hand when investigating the murders of Samantha and Jazmine Bisset. Various possible links were identified which pointed towards Robert Napper as a possible suspect for the Rachel Nickell murder but our approach to the Nickell investigation at Wimbledon was totally rebuffed and we were made to feel, far from being helpful, an imposition. At the time, the Wimbledon team had decided Colin Stagg was guilty of that murder. Any deviation from that mantra was dismissed out of hand. The last thing the Wimbledon investigators needed just at that particular time was (as they must have seen it) a rag tag team from south east London, who were investigating a murder few people had ever heard of, offering an alternative suspect in their high-profile job in which they had invested so much time and which was achieving daily saturation media coverage.

The same syndrome can pop up in smaller scale incidents within an investigation. This can lead to major decision blunders if not brought to heel. An example of this again featured during the Bisset investigation. A training shoeprint was lifted from within the crime scene at Heathfield Terrace. It was not a straightforward, clean shoeprint, but a composite of several fragments of the same shoe, some parts of which were made in blood, making it plain the prints were left after the murder. The fragments were painstakingly reconstructed and when complete examined by an expert. The expert estimated the trainers to be between size 8 and 9. A photograph of the print together with the shoe size was circulated to all police stations to be compared against any trainers worn by arrested burglars. Subsequently, more thought was given to the trainer size and, after more information of conditions at the scene and other fragments were found to add to the composite, further information was passed to the shoe experts who re-assessed the size as between 9 and 10. However the damage was done and for months afterwards I despaired at office meetings when the 'small' shoe size was mentioned as an eliminating factor, or even more bizarrely as possibly belonging to a female. Once an idea takes hold it is very difficult to dislodge it.

In any event, whichever way it was looked at, Colin Ash-Smith by his appalling attacks on two local women was certainly now a golden suspect. Unfortunately for the Kent murder team, he declined to play ball. After a lengthy interview and being confronted with forensic evidence he finally admitted both the attempted rape and attempted murder of Beverley Godfrey and the stabbing of Charlotte Barnard. But, to the frustration of the investigators he stubbornly refused to admit to any involvement in the murder of Claire Tiltman. Although the team were convinced Ash-Smith had murdered her, there was no evidence, forensic or otherwise to prove that he did. A confession was the only way to resolve the case.

Feelings were running high within the community of Greenhithe. The general feeling was that Ash-Smith had murdered Claire. This assumption was not suppressed by the police or the press, who by now had Colin Ash-Smith firmly in their sights. The rumour mill was operating in overdrive. The quiet life of the Ash-Smiths was to be changed forever. Diane found it impossible to carry on her duties as mayor and both she and Aubrey were exposed to an atmosphere in the British Legion Club so toxic they both had to leave. To add to their woes the press was building up its own campaign to prove the guilt of Colin Ash-Smith. One of the by-products of this was for Aubrey Ash-Smith to take it upon himself to find and destroy a knife which had belonged to his son as already described in *Chapter 11*. This foolish act of trying to protect his son had far-reaching ramifications and the reverse effect of the intentions of Aubrey, adding fuel to the fire of the school of thought that Colin was guilty of Claire's murder and being protected by his family.

However, the Ash-Smith family continued with their day-to-day lives, albeit interrupted by the waves of revulsion that everyone felt within the community. Diane and Aubrey both quit their posts as local councillors within days of Colin's arrest. Prior to her son's arrest Diane was very popular locally and had built up a reputation as someone who could get things done. Aubrey was also heavily involved in campaigning for the Labour party. They were both well known and easily approachable. They offered direct support to Linda and Cliff Tiltman who they also knew socially through all being members of the Greenhithe British Legion Club, which acted as a community centre. Diane and Aubrey's only son Colin was seen as awkward but harmless. He had always held down a steady job and only came to notice within the village through his ownership of his flashy white Ford Capri in which he was often to be seen driving within the environs of Greenhithe. As noted in earlier chapters, he had taken up with a quiet young woman, Stella Murrell and they lived together in a flat on the Ingress Estate where they seemed perfectly happy with no complaints from neighbours, work colleagues or anybody else. Colin could best be described as a very ordinary, introspective young man.

Apart from a natural interest in the investigation into the murder, the Ash-Smiths were never an important part of proceedings. As described in *Chapter 9*, Diane had attended the incident room together with the then Mayor of Greenhithe and Swanscombe, Philip Crow, to be apprised of the progress, the better to inform her constituents. Aubrey sympathised with the Tiltmans via their shared association at the British Legion Club and Colin had provided a witness statement in which he vaguely described a young person he had seen in London Road on the evening of the murder. Ash-Smith's statement was filed with many other such statements of only marginal assistance in the growing Tiltman dossier.

After the attack on Charlotte Barnard in October 1995 (two years and nine months after the murder of Claire) and the arrest of Colin, life changed radically for the Ash-Smith family. Disbelief was quickly followed by their being shunned which, in some cases, turned into personal verbal attacks. Their happy association with the British Legion became untenable and Diane and Aubrey both ceased going there as the atmosphere of suspicion grew. They had moved from their address in Milton Street prior to the events of October 1995. Colin had lived with them with Stella in Milton Street until his parents move in February 1995 to their new house closer to Dartford. At the time of this change, Stella and Colin moved into the flat at Beach Brow, Ingress Park.

Subsequent to the attack on Charlotte on October 17, Aubrey made a lengthy statement to police on October 19 which included many details of Colin's history, his school life, friendships and what had happened on the evening of the attack on Charlotte. Colin had visited the family home after attending his one-day milkman training course and then left, ostensibly to meet Stella at 6.15 pm. Aubrey and Diane had remained indoors for the evening until 9.30 pm when Diane went out to buy a fish and chip supper. After supper they went to bed at 1 am.

They were disturbed by a knock on their door at 2.20 am from a distraught Stella. Through the tears she told them Colin had been arrested for attempted murder. After telephoning various police stations they were unable to get any further information so drove down with Stella to Beach Brow. Diane had her own key to the flat and let herself in, only to be confronted by a police officer who prevented them from entering further. The officer was able to furnish them with further details of what had happened and in a state of shock they drove to Dartford Police Station. At the police station it was confirmed Colin had been arrested on suspicion of attempted murder and could not be seen. They decided to return home.

Aubrey also frankly told police how Colin did own a knife which had a six-inch blade. Aubrey hadn't seen this knife for six months or so. He had last seen it when he asked Colin for something to sharpen a pencil and Colin produced it from his jacket pocket. He told Colin he should not have such a knife in his possession. Aubrey had not seen the knife since. He confirmed that Colin was left-handed. Not unnaturally, Diane and Aubrey could not bring themselves to believe Colin could have committed such an act of violence. He had never shown any violence towards them and in fact it was quite the opposite, Colin always being helpful and on hand to help them or his grandparents. This type of situation is not in itself as unusual as the public might think and should not be used as proof, one way or the other, to demonstrate someone's violent nature.

On Friday 20 October 1995, Colin was charged with the attack on Charlotte and found himself on remand at HM Prison Elmley on the Isle of Sheppey. Aubrey went to visit him and asked Colin if it was true that he had attacked Charlotte. Colin couldn't find the words to reply to his father. He remained silent. It was only then Aubrey felt that the allegation *was* true, as Colin had never to his knowledge lied to him. It was only after being charged with the second offence, that of the attack on Beverley Godfrey, that Colin finally opened-up to his father. This was after Colin had asked for Stella and Diane to leave the room. Colin felt deeply ashamed and embarrassed talking about his offending in front of his mother. Colin admitted to Aubrey that he had attacked both Beverley and Charlotte.

Later, when Colin had been transferred to Broadmoor High Security Hospital for assessment, Aubrey visited him on his own, making the journey by himself with the specific aim of asking Colin about whether he had murdered Claire. Colin had a premonition as to why his father was visiting him. As soon as Aubrey entered the visiting area Colin said, 'You've come up here to ask me some things, haven't you?' Aubrey replied, 'Only if you want to tell me.' 'To which Colin replied, 'Dad, I've done nothing else and whoever killed Claire ought to be strung up.'

The Ash-Smiths were feeling the heat even more locally as almost the entire community turned against them. Oddly those who had lost the most, Linda and Cliff Tiltman were not so quick to join the growing chorus of opprobrium. They remained calm in such terrible circumstances and, although they both became convinced of the guilt of Colin Ash-Smith, they retained their dignity to the very end. Neither ever recovered from the shock of losing their beloved daughter. Linda died in 2008 and Cliff in 2012, both well before the trial of Colin Ash-Smith for their daughter's murder.

On Thursday 2 November 1995, Cliff Tiltman was in Dartford town centre when at 10 am outside the Post Office he bumped into Aubrey Ash-Smith. The meeting was entirely coincidental. The two men had known each other for eight years. Aubrey was walking towards Cliff when they said 'Hello' to each other. Cliff thought Aubrey looked upset so asked him, 'How are you?' Aubrey said, 'We've had a bit of a setback.' There was an awkward silence before Aubrey continued, 'I don't know if you know but they are going to charge my son with that attack in Swanscombe in 1988.'

Cliff replied 'No.' Aubrey, who had by now realised the implications of Colin possibly being responsible for Cliff's daughter's murder continued, 'I have spoken to Diane about it, and I have asked her where Colin was on the 18 January 1993, she says Colin was with her in the car when Claire was attacked.'

This is quite an extraordinary slice of drama on the High Street. One father of an accused murderer was opening his heart to the father of the victim his son was suspected of killing. Aubrey added, 'I don't know what to believe any more.' Cliff was left with the impression that Aubrey was unsure whether he was being told the truth by his wife Diane, however he was convinced that Aubrey was telling the truth when he said he knew nothing about the attack on Claire. Four days after this chance meeting Cliff told a police officer, 'I don't believe he knows anything about Claire's murder because, if he did, I think he would tell me.'

The investigation was now moving into its second phase. The absence of a suspect for the Claire Tiltman murder had been entirely filled by Colin Ash-Smith. The investigating team were re-galvanised into action. They had spent nearly three years since Claire's murder in frustrated gridlock and now the chance was on offer for them to close the Tiltman case. Without doubt, in anyone's eyes, Colin Ash-Smith fulfilled the role of the perfect suspect. Now it was the investigating team's job to work backwards and connect Ash-Smith to the scene of Claire's murder.

All of the original reports were pored over in the light of their new suspect. Even Mayor Philip Crow was called on to review his visit to the Northfleet incident room after Claire's murder, a visit which had included then Councillor Diane Ash-Smith. Crow was now disposed to put a slightly more sinister slant on the visit. He explained how they had been introduced to D Supt Owen Taylor and at the end of the meeting Taylor had asked if there were any questions. Crow now recalled Diane Ash-Smith asking 'probing questions' about the car parked in London Road with its hazard warning lights on. He also remembered feeling that the questions went beyond what he might term 'public interest'. He also felt the need to mention that Diane was 'particularly interested' in how vehicles were identified and eliminated by the police computer system. The whole culminated in a strange, lop-sided, formal statement to police.

Another matter which received particular attention was the forensic report of Dr Michael Heath who had attended the crime scene in the alleyway next to London Road and later performed the post mortem on Claire just before midnight on the night of 18 January 1993. Whilst carrying out his examinations at the scene and in the mortuary, Dr Heath made no reference as to the 'handedness' of the attacker. He attended Northfleet Police Station on Friday 29 January 1993 for a conference with D Supt Taylor at 12.15 pm. In his statement he says, 'I discussed with Det Supt Taylor the exact details and directions of the stab wounds.' The statement is dated as having been written on 3 March 1993, some six weeks after the murder. There is no significance to be attached to the delay in providing the post mortem report in statement fashion, it is common practice for a delay in these affairs.

Dr Heath and D Supt Taylor met to discuss the outcome of the post mortem. What is significant is that although Dr Heath describes the details and directions of the stab wounds, he at no point makes any deduction or opinion as to whether the assailant was left-handed or right-handed. He concluded his statement by listing the wounds, nine in total and all, with one exception, to the right-hand side of the victim's body. The wounds were consistent with being caused by a single edged cutting instrument. There were no defence wounds and death had been caused by multiple stab wounds.

As explained, earlier, it is customary where a defendant is charged with an offence of murder that their defence team will request a second, independent post mortem. If, as in this case, there is no defendant, the Crown appoints another pathologist to perform a second post mortem for the use of any subsequent defendant. On 9 February 1993, Dr Peter Jerreat took on the responsibility of this second post mortem at West Hill Hospital mortuary. Dr Jerreat broadly agreed with Dr Heath's findings and in his conclusion found that Claire had died from multiple stab wounds. However, he then added, 'The distribution and directions [of the stab wounds] suggested an assault from behind the deceased' adding 'there is very little evidence of any significant defence put forward by Claire Tiltman. This would confirm "the attack from behind" thesis.' Dr Jerreat followed Dr Heath in making no hypothesis on the handedness of the assailant. In the absence of a defendant, all so far so good.

Then on Tuesday 7 November 1995 (three weeks after the Charlotte Barnard attack and almost three years after Claire's murder) Dr Heath attended the police incident room at Dartford Police Station where he was in conference with senior officers from the Charlotte Barnard enquiry headed by D Supt Biddiss. He examined a knife exhibited as PB/4 on 7 November 1995. It was a bayonet with a blade 17.6 cm long and 2.1 cm wide. Aubrey Ash-Smith had handed it to police when they searched his house (then in Myrtle Place, Dartford) on the 22 October 1995. He had explained it belonged to his grandfather and was a war relic and had no connection to Claire's murder (This is exhibit PB/4 described more fully in the list of items seized by police later in this chapter). The knife used in the Charlotte Barnard attack and discarded by Ash-Smith near the Beach Brow address was marked Exhibit GDM/1. This was also found *not* to be the one used against Claire.

The old address of the Ash-Smiths in Milton Street was searched and another old bayonet which had been left behind when they departed the premises was handed over: CWR/1. It was conclusively shown that neither this, nor any of the knives in police possession, were used in the murder of Claire Tiltman. Another knife of interest was a sheath knife (Exhibit BPO/1). After admitting to the attack on Beverley Godfrey, Ash-Smith told police he had given the knife he had used in that attack to his friend Guy Hudson. Guy was asked about this and remembered he had left it at his old address when he moved out. The knife was found in a box under the stairs. Guy had moved prior to the murder of Claire and it was shown beyond doubt that BPO/1 was *not* used in her murder.

Dr Heath then examined: Claire's jacket (MJH/8) which she had been wearing when attacked on 18 January 1993; the notes he had made at the original post mortem; and photographs of her body, paying particular attention to her stab wounds. Turning his attention to Charlotte Barnard he examined photographs which displayed the stab wounds she had received during her attack by Ash-Smith. On Charlotte's back he found four groups of two stab wounds: two stab wounds over the back of the right side of the chest measuring 1.1 cm and 1.2 cm; two over the upper aspect of the left loin measuring 1.5 cm and 1.1 cm; two over the lower aspect of the right loin measuring 1.5 cm and 1.7 cm; two over the lower aspect of the left loin measuring 1 cm and 1 cm. In addition, there was a single horizontal stab wound over the lower posterior flank of the abdomen, measuring 1.3 cm. There was extensive bruising and stab wounds to the back of the right hand in classic defence wound style.

Later the same day Dr Heath attended the victim suite in Greenhithe where he examined Beverley Godfrey and Charlotte Barnard. After his examinations he came to the following conclusions (paraphrased):

- **Beverley Godfrey:** The healed stab wounds on Beverley's back were consistent with having been caused by a knife with a maximum blade width of 1.5 cm. There were no defence wounds on Beverley.

- **Charlotte Barnard:** The stab wounds were consistent with having been caused by a knife which measured up to 1.5 cm at the point of penetration. The wounds to the victim's back were caused by the assailant using the knife in a jabbing motion. The defence wounds indicated a sustained attempt to shield the body from being stabbed.

- **The overall pattern of stab wounds:** This indicated Charlotte had defended herself whilst face-to-face and on turning to the right had sustained the wound to her right side and then the jabbing wounds to her back. The pattern of injuries was entirely consistent with having been caused by a left-handed assailant. (A fact corroborated by the victim herself).

- **Claire Tiltman:** After consulting the post mortem photographs, his own original post mortem report and Claire's jacket, it became the opinion of Dr Heath that. 'Claire Tiltman was attacked by an assailant with a knife in his left hand. This indicates the assailant was left-handed.'

In his final conclusions, Dr Heath deduced that both Claire and Charlotte had been attacked by an assailant with a knife in his left hand, indicating the assailant was left-handed. He further concluded the pattern of injuries to both Claire and Charlotte showed marked similarities. In each case the initial assault had been sustained whilst the victim and assailant had been face-to-face and in each case the victim had then rotated to her right and finally sustained injuries to her back. The injuries to Beverley were consistent, but not diagnostic with having been caused by a left-handed person.

In the 'Life Maps' drawn and written by Ash-Smith many years later in prison Ash-Smith states that during the Beverley attack he actually swapped the knife from his right to his left hand and then pushed the knife into her five times whilst he held an air-pistol in his right hand. (Note he describes the stabbing action as 'pushed'. The subsequent medical examination substantiated this type of stab wound. Not the wild stabbing experienced by Claire). Whatever the research shows, there is absolutely no doubt that Colin Ash-Smith is and always has been left-handed.

Once Dr Heath had submitted his report the investigating team would have been extremely satisfied. The question of convicting Ash-Smith of attacking Beverley and Charlotte was never in doubt, but the big prize was to convict him of the murder of Claire. They were on their way to having some of the evidence they so desperately needed. A highly qualified forensic examiner had provided 'evidence' that, not only had Claire been attacked by a left-handed person (Ash-Smith) but that the two attacks on Charlotte and Claire showed 'marked similarities'.

No doubt a few moments of euphoria were experienced on receipt of this helpful result. However, let everybody take a step backwards. As has been mentioned, it is too easy to be caught up in the moment after what has, up until now, been an intractable problem that suddenly shows a glimmer of light. The investigating team were pleased with themselves. But were they at fault for confirming their own bias towards Ash-Smith being guilty of murdering Claire? Could it be that by staring too hard at Colin, with tunnel vision, they missed the real suspect on their peripheral horizon? It was at this point in the investigation that things appear to have taken a more slanted turn. As I will argue, everything from this moment on deserves careful scrutiny.

The attacks could not really be described as 'similar'. I agree they were all young women within a small geographical location who were alone and vulnerable. The serious injuries to Charlotte and Beverley were in no way as ferocious and brutal as the attack on Claire. It is also stretching it to say that Beverley was in a public place when she was kidnapped off her own driveway, outside her bungalow in the school grounds. To be clear, it is not the intention to diminish the fear and dreadful trauma Charlotte and Beverley suffered, they were without doubt in fear for their lives and could easily have ended up as fatalities. But the savagery of the attack on Claire does not bear the same hallmarks. Five of the knife-blows to her fragile frame would on their own have proved fatal. The wounds to Beverley and Charlotte, although serious, just were not in the same category. They did not to my investigative mind bear the same signature.

The fact is, the first time the 'handedness' of the assailant was ever openly considered was only *after* Ash-Smith found himself in custody and it became apparent he was left-handed. This I believe can only leave doubt as to the validity of any arguments subsequently put forward that Claire Tiltman's assailant was left-handed. Again, a dispassionate look at the scene of blood distribution and the positioning of the wounds on

Claire's body must be taken into account. In a surprise frontal attack with no offer of resistance it is difficult to establish from the positioning of the wounds whether the attacker was left-handed or right-handed. What is a known fact is the angle of inflection of the knife penetration. Of the nine wounds suffered by Claire, two were *vertical* (relative to the spine) and seven inflected *markedly to the left. None* had entry angles of inflection *to the right*. All of this makes determination of the handedness of the assailant difficult. At the very least, it leaves the handedness of the attacker very unclear. However, when you grip and point a knife at something it inflects in the *opposite* direction, meaning that seven of Claire's wounds point prima facie to a right-handed attacker. Simply put, when a left-hander grips a knife it inflects to the right, and when a right-hander does so it inflects to the left. It is a muscle contraction in the hand which causes this to happen. The complete scenario should be re-examined by an independent forensic expert.

It should be noted from what has already been said that Dr Jerreat concurred that the multiple stab wounds to Claire, by their direction and distribution suggested an assault from behind, not as Dr Heath now seemed to be postulating 'face-to-face'.

Taking everything into consideration from the accounts of both pathologists it would seem most likely Claire was attacked initially from a face-to-face aspect and then turned her back to flee. In his first post mortem report Dr Heath believed the first wound was the one which entered above her left breast and would have been from a position of face-to-face. This wound alone would have proved fatal. Six more wounds were inflicted to her right chest area whilst the assailant stood in front of the victim and the final two blows were from behind. This would fit with a scenario of the attacker concealing himself in the alleyway side steps which lead upwards to the doctors' surgery, jumping out and surprising Claire. The side steps are on the right side as you walk up towards Riverview Road and perform the function of a short cut to the surgery.

Claire, in shock, would have turned and fled back towards the main London Road pursued by her assailant who stabbed her again, this time twice in the back. One of those blows struck an artery and blood spattering, consistent with a knife being plunged in and out, was found on the wooden fence just before the alleyway exit to the main London Road. Claire staggered into the main road, collapsed and was immediately spotted by witnesses who saw no-one else, which would suggest the assailant made off up the alleyway towards Riverview.

This brings into focus the witness Christine Doyle mentioned in *Chapter 7*. To remind readers, she was a resident in Ivy Bower Close leading towards Riverview Road, opposite to the alleyway, who saw a male limping along, 'dragging a leg', and looking behind him having come from the direction of the alleyway. He was of medium build wearing a light-coloured jacket and, by her detailed description, wasn't Colin Ash-Smith.

CHAPTER 13

In Custody

From the moment Colin Ash-Smith was in custody his life effectively changed for ever. From an obscure, awkward young man living out his life as a milkman in a small Kent town, he had managed to engineer himself a new identity as a serial sexual predator. He had done this entirely of his own volition. He didn't have the usual excuses of a broken, unloved childhood. There was no evidence or history of abuse, he was raised in a close, comfortable, and stable family who had supported him through his adolescence and personal difficulties. He had found a young woman in Stella Murrell who also loved him.

It seems likely that Colin did suffer from a psychiatric disorder, which manifested itself in the attacks on Beverley and Charlotte. These alone were sufficient to ostracise him from the Greenhithe community for ever, even without the associated suspicion that he had murdered Claire Tiltman. He had an uncanny knack of being able to disguise this violent streak he harboured. This ability to shut out his dark side manifested itself most chillingly after the attack on Charlotte Barnard when, within minutes, he was back at home with Stella preparing to go out for the evening with friends at The Plough public house. There he displayed no outward signs whatsoever of any turmoil he may have felt for the terrible crime he had just committed.

The trait in his personality of being able to function coolly and dispassionately after committing traumatic crimes was to bring suspicion to bear on whether he was responsible for the murder of Claire Tiltman and how after that event he was able to calmly attend her funeral. Conversely, after his attack on Beverley Godfrey he had been filled with remorse. Incapable of attending work and even going so far as to telephone the police to admit to the crime, albeit anonymously. After the Charlotte Barnard assault and subsequent to his arrest he was incapable of telling his mother of his guilt such was his sense of shame. He preferred to confess all to his father in a meeting between just the two of them.

Just what drove him to commit these two dreadful acts will probably never be known. He did have a fascination with pornography, some of it extreme. He also had an infantile preoccupation with knives and had possessed at times some fearsome weapons. But what tipped him over the edge to commit such heinous acts is a mystery. One thing is for sure, he must have known if he was captured carrying out knife attacks on young women in the Greenhithe area he must fall under suspicion for the murder of Claire Tiltman.

His attack on Charlotte was so risky in the likelihood of him being discovered that it is almost laughable. The offence was within a few hundred yards of where he lived and he drove to the attack site in his own distinctive white Ford Capri, parking it across the road from the incident. The area where Charlotte was attacked was quite busy and not secluded, it was close to a railway station used by commuters which was constantly disgorging many daily travellers. The lack of planning prior to the offence was lamentable and would have been comical were it not so serious. He even dragged the unfortunate Charlotte across the road to what he thought was a secluded factory yard, only to find the gates locked.

It may be surmised that Colin Ash-Smith wanted to be caught. Either knowing of his own dark propensities and wanting to put a stop to them, or maybe desiring some kind of notoriety to divorce himself from the dull individual he undoubtedly was. Or he had reached the stage in his violent attacks on defenceless women where he believed he was invincible and would never be caught. This may go some way to explain the keeping of the tie in his car from the 1988 Beverley Godfrey attack. Whichever scenario is correct, without doubt the police and the population of Greenhithe were relieved at his arrest for the attacks on Beverley and Charlotte. It seems they also had no doubt that Colin Ash-Smith had murdered Claire.

Ash-Smith had overwhelming evidence against him for the attacks on Beverley Godfrey and Charlotte Barnard and the investigation now went into the phase which the police describe as 'being processed'. This involved him being formally charged with the attempted murder and attempted rape of Beverley Godfrey and the attempted murder of Charlotte Barnard. After being charged he appeared before a magistrate and was remanded in custody to await his trial. The police meanwhile set about firming up evidence against him to charge him with the 1993 murder of Claire Tiltman.

They reviewed the murder scene and the forensic evidence. They revisited all the important witnesses. No further evidence was forthcoming, with the one exception. The opinion of Dr Heath that whoever had attacked Claire had used their left hand to hold the knife and was *ipso facto* (my own words) left-handed. Their chief suspect Colin Ash-Smith was, without doubt left-handed in common with between 8% to 10% of the general population. Good circumstantial evidence but on its own and without an admission not nearly enough to charge anyone with murder.

The wheels of justice grind extremely slowly and the trial of Colin Ash-Smith for the attacks on Beverley and Charlotte was not until June 1996. During this time the police were unable to find any more evidence to substantiate their belief that he had murdered Claire. A belief which had quickly seeped into the minds of the local population of Greenhithe and the national press. So began the vitriolic and sustained attacks against his parents described in *Chapter 11*. Once knowledge of Aubrey Ash-Smith's rather pathetic attempt to pervert the course of justice was in the public domain the condemnation knew no bounds.

On his own admission, after Colin's arrest Aubrey had taken one of Colin's old knives and boiled it before breaking it in a vice and throwing away the pieces into some undergrowth. Aubrey confessed to police as to what he had done after he had been reported to them by someone who had overheard him talking about it in the pub. He had a reputation for enjoying his beer and on this occasion had let his mouth run away with him. The police arrested him and he immediately confessed, taking them to the spot where he had thrown the pieces away, which were all recovered. The knife was compared to Claire Tiltman's wounds and found without doubt *not* to have been the weapon that caused them.

Meanwhile the police had plenty to occupy themselves. With Ash-Smith in custody and a firm suspect for Claire's murder, consideration was given to strengthening evidence in the absence of a confession. During searches of his known addresses police seized a large quantity of items which were subsequently examined in detail. Amongst these items the most significant were:

- A number of knives.
- The clothing he was wearing during the attack on Charlotte. In particular, his jacket, which was forensically examined not only for evidence from the Charlotte Barnard attack but also for DNA traces from Claire Tiltman.
- A diary within which he had recorded his fantasies on attacking women and referred specifically to the attack on Beverley. The diary demonstrates just how dangerously far down the road of being a sexual predator Ash-Smith had wandered and how he needed to be arrested. However, it makes no reference to the Claire Tiltman attack which is odd as the diary is very egocentric and boastful of his 'achievements'. Within it he stakes a claim that the 1988 Beverley Godfrey attack was his 'MASTERPIECE'—but not a whisper of Claire.

The knives which *can* be attributed to Colin Ash-Smith are as follows and worth setting out in some detail:

- Exhibit GDM/1, the green handled flick knife found by PC Gary Marshall in the undergrowth outside Ash-Smith's flat in Beach Brow two days after the stabbing of Charlotte Barnard. As previously outlined, Ash-Smith had thrown it from his window when the police came calling on the night of his arrest. On forensic examination this knife was found to have fatty deposits and fibres on the blade which were attributable to Charlotte. This is rock solid evidence that GDM/1 belonged to Ash-Smith (confirmed by Stella) and it was used in the attack on Charlotte.

- The lock knife taken by Aubrey Ash-Smith who had then attempted to destroy and dispose of it. This was forensically examined and was quickly discounted as not having been used in any of the three assaults, having only a three-inch blade.

- Exhibit BPO/1, a sheath knife with an interesting history. This knife belonged to Colin before the Beverley Godfrey attack in 1988. At some time after using this knife to attack Beverley, Ash-Smith gave it as a gift to his friend Guy Hudson who put it into a box under the stairs at the Darenth house he then lived in. Hudson moved on but left the knife behind in its box. As a result of Colin's confession to the Beverley attack, police attended the Darenth address and spoke to the then current owner Brian Osbourne who looked under the stairs and found the knife where Guy Hudson had told them it would be.

- Exhibit PB/4, an old wooden handled bayonet which was owned by Aubrey Ash-Smith and handed over to police together with two model/replica handguns. One replica had been bought in Great Yarmouth whilst on a family holiday. The other, a replica revolver, had been given to him by his friend Hudson. The bayonet it transpired had belonged to Aubrey's grandfather who'd retained it as a war trophy. It was deemed 'highly likely', by forensic scientist Roger Mann, during his testing on 10 January 1996, that it could have made the cuts to Claire's jacket.

- Exhibit CWR/1, another bayonet which was left behind in Milton Street when the Ash-Smiths moved out. The new occupier handed it in to police after Ash-Smith's arrest. It was also discounted as being relevant.

Whilst on the subject of the knives, it should be mentioned that both BPO/1 and PB/4 were taken by forensic scientist Roger Mann on 10 January 1996 and compared with the stab holes in Claire's jacket. The logic is clear, to establish whether either knife could have been used in the attack on Claire. Mann concluded regarding bayonet PB/4, 'In my opinion ... it is highly likely that the bayonet, particularly in its present condition could have made the cuts in the jacket.' He then tested the sheath knife BPO/1 and concluded, 'It is my opinion that it could have made the stab-cuts present in Claire Tiltman's jacket.' Unfortunately, so could millions of other knives and as evidence this is virtually worthless. It should also be noted sheath knife BPO/1 was no longer in the possession of Colin Ash-Smith at the time of Claire's murder.

I do not know what form this so-called 'mechanical fit' took but it seems, looking back as a reviewer of the case, there is serious cause for concern on cross-contamination grounds. Police and scientists knew the knives had been in the possession of Ash-Smith and there was a danger they could accidentally introduce some of Ash-Smith's DNA via the knives to Claire's jacket. At the very least that scenario could be a future interpretation for any defence team.

There were other knives featured in this case, but none were thought to be significant. Ash-Smith's clothing, as worn during the attack on Charlotte, was subjected to forensic scrutiny, as was all his other clothing which he may have worn during the murder of Claire. This was the light-coloured jacket which Ash-Smith could be seen wearing at her funeral. This is also the description of a light-coloured jacket seen by various witnesses at or about the time of Claire being attacked, especially the 'light jacket' seen worn by an unidentified suspect by Christine Doyle, coming from the direction of the alleyway at around the time of the murder. This also resembles the jacket worn by Robert Napper in a photograph taken whilst he was under surveillance by police prior to his arrest on 27 May 1994 in Plumstead.[7]

---

7. The surveillance photo appears on page 184. It shows Napper wearing a jacket fitting the descriptions of several witnesses concerning one or more individuals they saw in the vicinity of Claire's murder.

Ash-Smith's jacket from the Barnard attack contained a wealth of DNA, blood and fibre traces from Charlotte connecting him to the assault. Not one iota of the same was found on any of his other seized clothing which may have linked him to Claire's murder. The 1988 ring bound 'steel stock' diary found at Beach Brow in Ash-Smith's room contained his explicit fantasies. It listed Ash-Smith's 'Assault Plans' (the bullet points are mine but the text is as per the original).

- **Assault Plan No. 1** 50% successful—Swanscombe railway station. Alone at a railway station, fully deserted apart from me AND a woman aged about 30 for about 25 minutes but I bottled it. It was late at night, all arrangements were made, where to take her, where to hide body, escape route, everything down to the last detail, but I bottled it—lucky for her I did I suppose.

- **Assault Plan No. 2** 50% successful—Stanhope Road. In full swing in my psycho state of mind, I had an alibi planned for between 7 and 3 pm in the evening. Rung up house to make sure husband was out, made way to back of her house, after 15 minutes via alleyway, broke into bathroom at back of house, made way into bathroom undetected, shredded a few clothes in laundry basket, just about to burst into front room when husband said something in room, made way out rather quickly undetected, a slight tactical retreat.

- **Assault Plan No. 3** 20% successful—Stanhope Road. At Old peoples home total abysmal failure rather not talk about.

- **Assault Plan No. 4** 95% successful—turned out to full Swanscombe Chalk Pits. [In the words of Ash-Smith] 'MY MASTERPIECE, also my last attack what wasn't planned'.

On this last assault Ash-Smith then goes into great written detail about how he carried out the attack. He tells the story in the first person which gives it an extra, chilling element. The attack without any doubt refers to Beverley Godfrey. He describes events and his victim in the finest detail which only the perpetrator would have known. He paints a picture of his victim's terror without any sign of it having any affect on him personally. He graphically details his frustration at not being able to raise an erection and blames the cold weather. He took Polaroid photographs of events, although he later claimed to have destroyed these and they have never been recovered to date. His remorse and cold cunning come into conflict as he describes how he made a 'snap' decision to kill Beverley, telling her, 'Sorry 'bout this but you've seen my face.' It was at this point he attempted to strangle her with his old school tie, but it snapped in two. He then took up his knife in his left hand and told her, 'I'm sorry but I can't do this.'

Ash-Smith then stabbed her five times in her back in a cross shaped pattern. The stab wounds were not frenzied in nature and were described by Beverley herself as 'push' wounds. He then collected his belongings together and covered what he believed was the dead body of Beverley in some leaves and ran for it back to his parents' house, reaching home at about 6 am and going to bed. After two hours he felt ill, threw up in his sink and decided not to go into work. He lay in his bed listening to the sirens of police cars in the distance and turned on his TV to watch the incident relayed on the news. It was only then he discovered Beverley had survived the attack. His reaction was, 'Damn she survived.'

Ash-Smith soon realised the police had recovered a part of his old tie and thought how lucky he was because the part he still had had his name on it. He hid his knife and air-pistol in some nearby woods and waited until the trail had gone cold before recovering them. He had committed the Beverley Godfrey attack in the early hours of 21 December 1988 and after spending the day at home he telephoned Joyce Green Hospital where Beverley was being treated. The call was forwarded to Dartford Police. The original message is timed at 7.22 pm. The caller (Ash-Smith) said, 'Are you looking for the bloke who stabbed that girl?'

Reply, 'Yes.'

Caller, 'I'm him. I tied her hands and legs up and stuffed tissue paper in her mouth.'

Reply, 'Will you give me your name?'

Caller, 'No. I'm getting on a train now to Charing Cross.'

The call then ended abruptly.

This document gives a rare and chilling insight into the mind of a person in the grip of his own fantasy world. It would be tempting to describe it as psychotic paranoia, but we must remember that Colin Ash-Smith's assessment at Broadmoor Hospital found him *not* to be mentally ill. It does however demonstrate the immature side to Ash-Smith's nature. Also, a cold cunning which his thought processes allowed him to believe it justifiable to take someone's life in order to protect his own identity.

This event in Ash-Smith's life does very little to endear him to the mind of any reader. It also beggars the question, did he really manage to control his criminally sexual urges for approaching seven years, until the attack on Charlotte Barnard? Case studies and history tell us this is highly unlikely.

CHAPTER 14

The Pressure Mounts on the Police and CPS

The investigating team put together their case for the Crown Prosecution Service in readiness for the forthcoming trial of Colin Ash-Smith. They had a cast iron case against him for the attacks on Charlotte and Beverley, ably assisted by Ash-Smith's confessions in full to those terrible crimes. Frustratingly however, evidence was not forthcoming for the case against him for the murder of Claire Tiltman. Ash-Smith had voluntarily attended police identity parades where he had been picked out by both Beverley Godfrey and Charlotte Barnard. He had also been identified by witnesses who had seen him close to the attack on Charlotte. Unfortunately for the police, not one of their witnesses who had seen a man behaving suspiciously just before and immediately after the Claire Tiltman attack were able to pick him out.

Whilst the search for evidence to connect him to the Tiltman case continued, Ash-Smith was arraigned at the Central Criminal Court (better known as The Old Bailey) for the offences against Beverley and Charlotte. The trial began on 24 June 1996 when he duly pleaded guilty to each of those two attacks. The suspicions against him of being the murderer of Claire would not and could not be taken into account and on 21 December 1996 he was sentenced to life imprisonment when the judge also imposed a minimum tariff of 15 years. The court appearance attracted frenzied activity from the media, all hungry for any news or evidence that connected the defendant to Claire Tiltman's murder.

Colin Ash-Smith entered the prison system leaving behind his shattered and distraught parents to face the onslaught of abuse from sections of the public. He also left the parents of Claire Tiltman convinced he was the killer of their only child. Ash-Smith had begun his time on remand on the Isle of Sheppey at HM Prison Elmley. He was transferred to HM Prison Belmarsh (close to his Kent home) on 24 October 1995 and remained there until the 20 January 1997 when he was transferred to HM Prison Wakefield. There then followed a series of moves to different prisons around the country including, Maidstone, Whatton and Lincoln until on 13 February 2014 he was returned to Belmarsh.

As already intimated, after Colin's arrest on 18 October 1995 the lives of the Ash-Smiths went into freefall. As described in *Chapter 11,* Diane had been elected a Labour councillor in 1988 and taken her duties to heart, becoming the consummate politician. So highly was she thought of that she was re-elected in 1992 which led to her becoming Mayor of Swanscombe and Greenhithe in May 1995. Aubrey was also a long serving councillor. Both were active members and fund raisers for the British Legion Club in Greenhithe where they were involved in organizing social events. With the arrest of Colin, in 1995 they decided to formally resign from the council and Diane as mayor. She, especially, received many letters of support from both Labour and Conservative members. However, they both felt they could not efficiently carry out their duties with the looming prospect of the trial of Colin for serious sexual offences against women. Meanwhile the investigation was gathering pace and the groundswell of public opinion was turning against them.

They continued to attend their beloved British Legion Club where they had both been members since the early 1980s. However, the atmosphere became ever more toxic. They were increasingly shunned by other club users until it reached the point when they ceased to go there. This was followed up by a letter addressed to them both from the club asking them to no longer visit and to resign their membership, 'because of the ill-feeling caused by their presence'. They both abided by the club's decision until, one evening, Aubrey decided to attend the club using his affiliated Working Mens' Club card. This precipitated an immediate response in the form of a letter from the legion banning him completely from the club.

Diane continued to work as a cab controller for All Night Cabs, a firm in Dartford, a job she really enjoyed and where she was well-respected. All of her work colleagues supported her, unfortunately this support was not carried over to the customers and she was regularly abused over the telephone and also by some visitors, usually drunk, to the cab office who hurled insults at her. On one occasion she was even spat upon. None of these attackers were known personally to Diane. The cab firm nevertheless continued their support for her and asked Diane to stay.

The constant reminder of what Colin had or might have done was not confined to work. Diane was receiving threatening telephone calls on her home telephone, the number of which was in the public domain through her work as a councillor. The calls were always anonymous and accused her of being a liar and even a murderer. It is a phenomenon of this type of case, one which achieves high-profile press coverage, that it often brings out the very worst in people. Usually, people who have no direct involvement in the case and who have decided through press reports and public house chatter not only to form their own opinions but to express them in the vilest manner. It is tragi-comic to watch these ill-informed 'upholders of justice' as they rush forward and beat the sides of prison vans or shout abuse in court. All the while convinced of their absolute right to commit such pathetic acts.

Diane did not resign from her job at the cab office and decided, despite never knowing when or where the next attack might be coming from, to continue working. This is not to say there were not moments of kindness. On one occasion Diane was with Stella shopping in the Co-op in Dartford. By now she was constantly on her guard from being approached by strangers who felt it was their duty to accost her on behalf of 'justice'. In this instance the lady behind the till looked up and said, 'Aren't you that Mrs Ash-Smith?'. Diane immediately bridled and curtly responded, 'Yes.' The shop assistant said, 'Just to say I feel terribly sorry for you.' Diane was shocked and moved in equal measures. Aubrey suffered more openly and could not adjust from being a pillar of the community to being the object of scorn and downright hostility.

Meanwhile the extended family of the Ash-Smiths took the decision to distance themselves from Diane and Aubrey. This was especially so in the case of Aubrey who found himself ostracised from his siblings and their children. From an initial standpoint of disbelief of what had happened, the realisation that their only son was guilty of being a sexual predator gradually dawned upon them. They shrank into defensive mode together with Colin's girlfriend Stella who came to live with them. Long discussions were held about what to do, and how they could best help Colin. They had heard that the police were interested in all of Colin's knives and had already seized some. Diane remembered another knife which was kept in a bowl on the windowsill. This is the knife first mentioned in *Chapter 11*. Although it only had a three-inch blade it did have an army khaki green-type handle. Diane said to Aubrey. 'For Christ's sake get rid of that bloody knife.' This was more out of frustration with the constant pressure from police and the investigators' obvious disbelief in the Ash-Smith story of being indoors with Colin on the night of Claire's murder.

Aubrey took Diane at her word and so boiled the knife, then broke it up and threw away the pieces. One of the effects of the pressure on Aubrey was to make him drink more and more. During one of his drinking bouts, he let slip in the pub about what he had done with it. This information was filtered back to the police who promptly arrested him for attempting to pervert the course of justice.

Aubrey immediately admitted what he had done and took police to where he had dumped the pieces which were all recovered. The upshot of this ill-advised action was that Aubrey found himself in custody and later convicted and sentenced to a year in prison. The sentence was not suspended, and Aubrey found himself a serving prisoner at HM Prison Elmley. This was seized upon by the press who followed the story closely in local newspapers fuelling the suspicions of the complicity of the Ash-Smiths in Claire's murder.

Diane was left in the unfortunate position of both her son and husband being in prison. Aubrey's sentence was followed by other social clubs with which he had been involved demanding his resignation, including a club he had been with for many years, Glentworth Ex-servicemen's Club.

Attitudes were now cementing even more unfavourably towards the Ash-Smiths. The police were now more than ever convinced that they were telling lies over Colin's alibi on the night of Claire's murder and did not hold back in telling Diane she was a liar. Colin had pleaded guilty on 24 June 1996 to assaulting and attempting to murder Beverley and Charlotte and was due to appear at the Central Criminal court on

21 December 1996 for sentencing. There was no trial as such as he was pleading guilty to one case of attempted murder, one case of attempted rape, one case of kidnap and one case of grievous bodily harm (GBH).

Diane was advised by the court not to attend. Nevertheless, she and Aubrey did go to watch her son plead guilty and be sentenced to life imprisonment for the attacks on Charlotte and Beverley along with his minimum tariff of 15 years. The pressure on the Ash-Smiths was relentless. They were constantly being door-stepped by members of the press looking for angles to sell their newspapers. This culminated in a letter delivered to Diane from a company called ITV Meridian as I will describe in the next chapter.

CHAPTER 15

The Deck is Stacked

Although Colin Ash-Smith was in prison, the general feeling that he had 'got away' with murder was very much the view of the vast majority of the population of Greenhithe and the case was still attracting an enormous amount of media interest. In 1997, ITV Meridian saw an opportunity to revisit the tragedy. Using the catchy title *A Mother's Love* they came up with the idea of comparing the two most affected women of the Tiltman tragedy, Linda Tiltman and Diane Ash-Smith.

The programme was headed by reporter Jonathan Marland whose approach to Diane was along the lines of how they (ITV Meridian) wanted to present her side of the story as it affected the 'loss' of her son. Somehow, they managed to persuade her to appear on camera and give her version of how the misdemeanours of her son had undermined her own life. According to Diane the reporter did not inform her that the police were aware of the programme, or that the premise was to compare her loss with that of Linda Tiltman. A shaky premise in what some may feel to be questionable taste. She was also told that she would be able to view the programme before it was broadcast (a not infrequent but somewhat vague and casual media 'assurance' I believe).

Whatever, having agreed to appear in the programme, her story was then held up in comparison to Linda Tiltman's about how she had lost her only child. Naturally, in reality the sympathy was heavily loaded towards Mrs Tiltman. At first all went well, it appeared to be exactly how the production company had explained what they were trying to achieve. As the filming progressed it became apparent that all was not as it seemed. Marland, spotting Colin's white Ford Capri, which was still parked on the drive of the Ash-Smith's house, asked if he could use it in his film, by driving around Greenhithe. Diane refused this request claiming the car was no longer in working order. Not to be deterred, the programme makers then went to the extent of hiring a lookalike white Ford Capri in which the reporter, Marland was filmed by a TV crew driving around in the vicinity of the murder as Ash-Smith may allegedly have done. A supposition for which there is absolutely no evidence (see *Chapter 17*).

The reporter is then seen 'doorstepping' Ted Wells (the constituent Diane visited on the evening of the murder) and his wife. He questioned them as to whether Colin and Diane actually did drop off leaflets at his house on the night of the murder. Ted Wells had already spoken at length to the police and, almost three years after the incident, could not confirm on which night Diane called. In fact, Diane claims she had only dropped the letter through the letter box and had not spoken to Wells. After such a passage of time his memory was hazy. To add to this, Wells was an elderly man who seems to have been suffering from worsening memory loss. For which he said on camera that he was receiving medication.

Whilst being interviewed for ITV Meridian, Diane admitted asking Aubrey to get rid of the small knife which had led to Aubrey's conviction for attempting to pervert the course of justice as described in *Chapter 11*. On the strength of this throwaway line she found herself arrested the morning after the programme aired. The police arrived at the Ash-Smith's house without warning at 8 am, just as Diane was preparing to make her weekly Wednesday journey to visit Aubrey in HM Prison Elmley.

Diane Ash-Smith was arrested for the same offence her husband had been convicted of, i.e. attempting to pervert the course of justice. This was described in the *Gravesend Reporter* on 28 August 1997 after which the news was quickly picked up by the national press, including *The Times* and *Independent*. One newspaper announced: 'Mother who admitted perverting the course of justice in an astonishing TV confession has been arrested' (No pre-judgement there then?). She was released on police bail until she was charged on 24 October 1997 and bailed to appear at Dartford Magistrates' Court. The case against her dragged on through various appearances and adjournments until eventually on the 21 May 1998 she appeared at Maidstone Crown Court where a trial date was set for 7 September 1998. Aubrey completed his prison sentence and was released in January 1998. In time to be at his wife's side as she went through the same process. With her it was taking much longer as she had entered a plea of not guilty.

Meanwhile Stella Murrell was still being pressured from all sides. Although she had genuine feelings for Colin, she felt as if she was being pushed. There was talk of marriage and this was coupled with antipathy from her own family, particularly her father. Despite his protestations and as described in *Chapter 10* she did marry Colin Ash-Smith. The ceremony was performed in Wakefield Prison on 27 May 1997. On 1 May 1997 an article had appeared in the *Sun* newspaper, ostensibly reflecting the views of Stella's father, who told the reporter of his 'anguish' over the prospect of his daughter's plans to marry a jailed 'maniac' suspected of killing schoolgirl Claire Tiltman. The marriage did not last as Stella found it increasingly difficult living with her in-laws under the constant strain of the knowledge her husband was in prison for sexual offences on women and suspicion that he may have killed Claire. Eventually, after two years, Stella left the Ash-Smith home and shortly afterwards sued for a divorce.

Although Stella found some happiness and remarried, her life was cut short by cancer. She died in July 2014, a short time before the Ash-Smith murder trial began. Stella had come forward to try and help police in their investigation of the murder of Claire and she was well aware they viewed Colin as their only suspect. She strived to always do the right thing and found herself unfairly caught up in a series of tragic events over which she had no control and through her naïvety only limited understanding.

Eventually, on 7 September 1998, Diane appeared for her trial at Luton Crown Court. It lasted for two days, during which she took to the witness stand and explained how she had no intention of hampering the police in their enquiries. She gave the explanation that she was convinced the knife had no relevance to the enquiry, but her husband Aubrey was obsessed with it. Eventually in frustration she had turned to him and told him to get rid of it. She explained further that if she had thought she'd done something wrong or committed an offence she would hardly have gone on TV to talk about it (a reference to the Meridian programme *A Mother's Love*).

Two days later she was acquitted by the jury. Diane Ash-Smith showed courage to stand by her convictions and plead not guilty to the charge when it would have been easy to have just entered a guilty plea and accepted what in all probability would have been a suspended sentence. Her supposition that the knife had nothing to do with her son's offences was later proved to be correct. This experience, coupled with that as a seasoned politician makes it seem strange that the defence at Colin's later murder trial made the decision *not* to call her as a witness. This decision will be explored later, for that explosive development was still 16 years away.

Another interesting, apparently unconnected, development popped-up during this frenetic time in the lives of the Ash-Smiths. On 19 April 1998 an article appeared in the *Sunday Times* under the headline 'Police link Nickell murder to serial killer'. It revealed how the police were considering that the murderer of Rachel Nickell was someone who had committed a series of 'murder clusters' involving 21 deaths, any one of which could not be ruled out as having been committed by Rachel's killer. The article was followed the next day in *Kent Today* under the headline 'Claire's murder; is it one of four?' which detailed possible links between her murder and that of Rachel Nickell. This theme ran on as a news item well into May detailing the issues raised by a police review team which was re-examining the Nickell murder. It included such quotes as appeared in the *Daily Express*, 'Detectives are probing the possibility that the same person could be responsible for the unsolved murders of Rachel Nickell and Claire Tiltman'. A spokesman for the Tiltman investigation said, 'We were in contact with the Rachel Nickell murder room very soon after Claire's death, so the news that the murders were similar is nothing new to us.'

Let us consider for a moment a few salient issues:

- The 'review' was not a murder review as we understand it today. The Cold Case Murder Review Group was not set up until 2000. Prior to its inauguration, reviews were chancy affairs and depended more on social and political pressures than any drive to solve outstanding crimes. The review referred to was probably 'Operation Enigma' which was conceived to utilise modern technology in an attempt to discern patterns of serial sex-offenders and murderers, the better to link their crimes by comparing geography, modus operandi, etc.

- The idea that the Nickell and Tiltman murders could have been committed by the same person was sound. The type of attack in both cases was similar, with some obvious inconsistencies. Claire was killed in the dark in winter, Rachel in the middle of the day in summer. Rachel a mature woman in the company of a child. Claire little more than a child herself.

- Now the real bugbear. In 1998 the Rachel Nickell team were on the back of a 'mauling' following the halting of the trial of Colin Stagg which led to the humiliation of the police investigating team. However, I can personally confirm that the enquiry team, despite the acquittal of Colin Stagg, still firmly believed at this time that Stagg was responsible.

- In the 'early stages' of the Tiltman enquiry the Kent Police investigators had looked at the murder of Rachel and having done so were assured by the Metropolitan Police Nickell investigating team that they had their man, i.e. Stagg.

- That team also looked at Robert Napper subsequent to his arrest in 1994 for the murders of Samantha and Jazmine Bisset in Plumstead in November 1993. Napper was dismissed as a suspect for Claire's murder because of a lack of similarity and that his offences were confined to south east London. Their research also showed him to be in prison at the time of Claire's murder.

How bizarre, how contraire, that without knowing it they would have been on the right track. If only they had stepped outside their 'confirmation bias' and looked at other possibilities. Meanwhile the suspect on which the Wimbledon murder team concentrated their resources was Stagg. The real culprit in the Nickell case wasn't going to surface until 2007, for we know now Napper did murder Rachel, miles from his supposed 'home' ground and in an attack that bore no obvious hallmarks of the Bisset murders. Also, and most alarmingly, Napper was *not* in prison at the time of Claire's death on 18 January 1993, he had been released early, just before Christmas 1992. Three weeks before Claire's murder took place.

CHAPTER 16

The Police Believe They Have Their Man

'It is a capital mistake to theorise before you have all the evidence. It biases the judgement.'— Sir Arthur Conan-Doyle's Sherlock Holmes (1905)

With Colin Ash-Smith still in prison, serving a life sentence for the attacks on Beverley Godfrey and Charlotte Barnard the pressure was put upon him to admit that he had also attacked Claire. This he steadfastly refused to do. Life went on in Greenhithe where Claire's parents continued to suffer their unimaginable loss. They continued with their calm dignity but could never escape the suspicion that Colin had murdered their daughter. This suspicion was fuelled by the press, the local feelings on the matter and not least by the undisguised attitude of the police toward Ash-Smith's guilt.

In January 1995 on what should have been Claire's 18th birthday a memorial bench was erected to her memory in a small memorial garden in Horns Cross, near to her family home (not to be confused with the small memorial plaque at the alleyway entrance in London Road: see below). This was followed by the *Kent Today* newspaper offering a £1,000 reward for any information which would lead to the identification of the murderer. No further clues had emerged to provide evidence as to who was responsible for her death. Various suspects from around the UK had briefly entered and exited the frame, including brief interest in Alan Conner who was suspected of a string of sexual offences in Wales and southern England. Conner committed suicide in Huntingdon, Cambridgeshire after admitting raping and murdering a chambermaid in Devon. The Kent investigators travelled to Huntingdon but could find nothing to link Conner with the Tiltman enquiry.

This state of limbo continued until the breakthrough came with the attack on Charlotte and arrest of Ash-Smith on 17 October 1995. In the meantime SIO, D Supt Owen Taylor, became seriously ill and was forced to resign from an active part in the investigation. His position was taken over by D Supt Biddiss who successfully prosecuted Ash-Smith for the attacks on the two women which had occurred on either side of Claire's death. As already noted, Ash-Smith was sentenced to life imprisonment for those offences in December 1996.

The sentencing of Ash-Smith brought speculation about the Tiltman enquiry to a new level with intense reporting by the media, all pointing the finger at him. Things became so heated that his mother, Diane broke her silence and issued a statement to the press in which she reaffirmed her belief that her son had not killed Claire. She was quoted as saying, 'My son is not capable of murder.' A not unnatural response from a mother, but it did nothing to relieve the weight of suspicion on her and her husband Aubrey. The consensus being that Colin Ash-Smith had been convicted of one attempted murder, kidnap, attempted rape and GBH with intent so could hardly be viewed in the light of being incapable of carrying out such an attack.

Diane's plea was followed by Aubrey writing to the *Kentish Times*. In this letter he pointed out that his son, prior to his convictions for assaulting Beverley and Charlotte, had no previous convictions for any crime whatsoever, violent or otherwise. He also made clear that at the time of Claire's murder Colin was never considered as a suspect. This plea was dramatically undermined when Aubrey was arrested for attempting to pervert the course of justice on 21 November 1995 at his home address in Stone, later convicted and imprisoned as described earlier in this book. This was the same incident over which Diane became embroiled when she admitted, during the ITV Meridian documentary, that she 'knew what Aubrey had done' (see *Chapter 15*) .

Five years after the murder another memorial was opened for Claire near to the entrance to the alleyway in London Road where she had been murdered in 1993. At the request of the Tiltman family the plaque included the name of D Supt Owen Taylor who had since succumbed to his illness and died. At the next anniversary, in January 1999, a ceremony was held when the ashes of Claire were finally buried at the request of her parents. This ceremony was carried out at St Mary's Church, Greenhithe, almost opposite to where Claire was killed.

In the year 2000 fresh hope was raised over the progress the science of DNA was making and in May of that year an announcement was made that these advances would be applied to the Claire Tiltman case. Again, a flurry of interest came to nothing and the hopes of the Tiltmans were dashed yet again. After this, the enquiry really did slump, much to the frustration of the Tiltmans. Nothing happened to boost matters until the situation was again rejuvenated, this time by the introduction of the Criminal Justice Act 2003. The Act introduced into English law for the first time the ability for prosecutors, in specified circumstances, to introduce evidence of the 'bad character' of an accused person, and for this to be put before a jury charged with weighing that person's guilt or innocence. The new rule came with various caveats so that it only applied in limited circumstances.

Also in 2003, on the 10th anniversary of Claire's death the *Dartford Times* ran an article which was critical of Kent Police. Cliff and Linda Tiltman were quoted as having said a TV reconstruction of the murder had been blocked and described how they'd been ignored by the new police team investigating the murder. The newspaper appealed to 'the people of Dartford and to prisoner X, to help ... find the killer of Claire.' Prisoner X was it can be assumed a thinly disguised nod towards Colin Ash-Smith who as this book describes many people had already decided was responsible for Claire's murder. If the public were in any doubt as to who X might be, they only had to read on to find the one and only suspect named as Ash-Smith then currently in HM Prison Wakefield. The newspaper appealed directly to Ash-Smith to come forward with any information he may have about Claire's death. This appeal provoked no response from Ash-Smith other than a private reassurance to his parents that he had not murdered Claire and would never admit to something he had not done.

Police responded publicly a few months later by repeating their hope that the advances in DNA would result in evidence against the murderer. This was followed in 2005 by a statement from them that forensic tests on items from the scene of the murder had not provided any useful leads. The rift between the police and the Tiltman family had been repaired and Cliff announced that police now visited him regularly with updates on the progress of the enquiry.

After the attempted rape, attempted murder and GBH with intent convictions of Colin Ash-Smith and the ensuing furore over the conviction of Aubrey and trial of Diane, where she was found not guilty, interest in the Tiltman case quietened down as far as the press were concerned. Until, on the fifteenth anniversary of her death in January 2008 when there was another attempt to rekindle interest in the story. The police had kept the case open and recent success in the Rachel Nickell case by leading forensics expert Professor Angela Gallop gave new impetus to what could be achieved with advances in DNA evidence. The Tiltman case was now under review by the Kent Police Cold Case Review Team which was modelled on the Metropolitan police's now well-established Murder Review Team.

It was in 2008 that a decision was made within Kent Police to subject the Tiltman murder to a cold case review. By this time D Supt Biddiss had retired, but not unnaturally he was consulted by the review team. Biddiss had conducted his own, as he described it, 'informal review' which had resulted in a fairly brief report that had been filed within the Kent Police's Specialist Crime Department. D Supt Biddiss' review covered the following points.

1. The crime scene for the murder had been seriously contaminated because the incident had been initially treated as a road traffic accident. It was not until the ambulance personnel removed her upper clothing to administer CPR that the stab wounds were located.
2. Cliff Tiltman was never formally eliminated from the enquiry. The family should always be eliminated as a matter of course.
3. There was a ship docked at Greenhithe Wharf at the time. The crew of the ship were never traced and identified.

Point No. 1 has some merit, but the scene was identified as a murder scene fairly quickly. However, this was after various outsiders had trampled on it. Given that the first duty in such circumstances is the preservation of life, the ensuing contamination is maybe understandable. In hindsight perhaps more could have been done to preserve the crime scene for a more thorough forensic examination. Especially for possible shoeprints.

On the second point that Cliff Tiltman should have been formally eliminated, this is in truth academic, and he was never, even on the most extreme hypothesis, ever considered to be suspect. The third point is also academic. Identifying the names of the crew of the ship docked at Greenhithe could be viewed as an oversight, but the reality is the area teemed with people in transit. Lorry and van drivers alone would have been in their hundreds.

Nick Biddiss demonstrated his commitment to the investigation at all levels. He was the classic detective, cross-referencing all information and double-checking crime scenes. He sanctioned and insisted that Ash-Smith's white Ford Capri be sent to Aldermaston laboratory for forensic examination, leaving no stone unturned in his pursuit of evidence. When asked about the return of some exhibits to the Ash-Smith family, he was adamant he had never agreed to any of these being returned to them. The only exhibits he sanctioned the disposal of were some intimate photographs taken by Ash-Smith of Stella and Ash-Smith himself. He authorised this to avoid any unnecessary embarrassment to Stella and her family. His personal view was that Colin Ash-Smith remained the principal suspect for the murder of Claire Tiltman. He also believed Ash-Smith to be a very dangerous man. It would be difficult to criticise him for this latter viewpoint.

During the review, Biddiss was asked about a message received from the Metropolitan Police which advised him that a serving prisoner, Mark Whistler, had informed them that Ash-Smith had confessed to Whistler whilst they were both on remand at HM Prison Belmarsh. The confession was that Ash-Smith had killed Claire. Biddiss was surprised on hearing this information and declared he had no recall of it whatsoever. He was adamant that such information would have been prioritised and dealt with immediately. He added that it was the first time he had ever been informed that Ash-Smith might have admitted the offence to anyone.

D Sgt David Brittain was traced in the Metropolitan Police and confirmed he did send such a fax but did not speak to anyone personally. This curious incident came at a time when the investigating team were hoping to introduce evidence via what is termed, within the legal system, a 'cell confession'. Such evidence is dubious at the best of times because prisoners have so many personal incentives to provide questionable accounts, not least early release or improved conditions. Hence the courts (unless such testimonies are convincing and can be fully corroborated) do not like using them. Nevertheless, apart from the mysterious Mark Whistler, other 'inside information' was sought. Three other prisoners were trying to be helpful. The first such help was given in 1997 by a Prisoner B (I have withheld his name) who met Ash-Smith at Belmarsh in January 1997. The conversations B had with Ash-Smith often related to past offences and B relayed an accurate account of the offences for which Ash-Smith had been convicted. Ash-Smith was asked directly by B, 'Why do they want to interview you about Claire's murder?' Also privy to this conversation was another prisoner, Prisoner W. Ash-Smith replied, 'I was in the area at the time and I am left-handed.'

Colin Ash-Smith went on to explain, 'I was with my mother that night, but much later in the evening.' He did not say at what time 'much later' was. He also told B he had driven his mother to a friend's house and waited for her outside the address. Whilst waiting he added that he had 'the urge to go and find another victim.' But, as he was about to drive off, his mother came out of the friend's house and got back in his car.

Later that same day Ash-Smith was in his cell with prisoner B and without any prompt said, 'I killed the girl.' He made no reference to who he meant. Prisoner B made a written statement to police and it remained in the police files. Before prisoner B could be asked about this information prior to Ash-Smith's trial for the murder of Claire he died, in June 2005. Prisoner W who had been privy to the conversation along with prisoner B was approached much later and made a statement to the police on 27 August 2013. This was some 16 years later.

Prisoner W remembered both Prisoner B and Ash-Smith with whom he sometimes played chess. He stated,

> 'I have been asked if I remember any conversations that took place in my cell with Prisoner B and Colin Ash-Smith, where Colin admitted to killing a girl. This simply did not and could not have happened. I never remember Colin talking about killing people with knives. This is the sort of thing that would stick in your mind, and if someone who was so quiet had said this, I would remember this.'

This later statement by prisoner W poured cold water onto the previous 'cell confession' theory and, with Prisoner B being deceased, police were left with only the statement of Ash-Smith's fellow prisoner Stefan Dubois to use as some form of cell confession. Dubois' statement fell well short of a confession, but was claimed to be and held up as such by the prosecution. Dubois, a close friend of Ash-Smith, made the statement on 4 February 2013. His friendship with Ash-Smith even extended to visiting him in prison after Dubois had been released. Dubois was at pains to explain that he had discussed offences with Ash-Smith but he had never knowingly discussed any offences which Ash-Smith had not been convicted of.

The one thing which was to get the prosecution team excited was Dubois' mention of Ash-Smith relaying a story to him on one occasion about how the latter was out in his Capri and feeling angry about something. Dubois remembered Ash-Smith saying he had seen someone on a zebra crossing and shortly afterwards 'snapping and attacking them'. Dubois could not be sure of the context in which this was told to him, or whether Ash-Smith was walking or driving.

The investigating team honed-in on mention of 'a zebra crossing', despite knowing that Dubois was making this statement recalling a conversation that had happened ten years previously in HM Prison Wakefield. Also, Dubois from his own admission was under strong medication at the time. Nevertheless, it was the mention of the zebra crossing that excited the investigators. However, in the rest of the statement, Dubois is clear Ash-Smith never made any admission of attacking or killing Claire. Ash-Smith was aware of the statement to police made by Dubois and he even spoke to him about it on the phone. A conversation which, as a category A prisoner was tape-recorded. Ash-Smith did not seem in the least concerned or anxious by his friend Dubois telling this story to the police and their friendship continued.

The time continued to slip by as Ash-Smith continued his life in various prisons and the population of Greenhithe continued to speculate on his awkward and disappointing refusal to admit to Claire's murder. By 2012, a new SIO, D Supt Rob Vinson[8] had taken over what was now a very cold case enquiry. There was still a great deal of interest locally which was channelled into trying to prove Ash-Smith had murdered Claire. Several of her school friends from 1992 formed an action group, their aim being to ensure the enquiry was not allowed to falter. The 'schoolgirls' were now young women with families of their own and they were committed as a group to pushing the investigation in memory of not only their friend Claire but also those of Cliff and Linda Tiltman. In March 2008 Linda died leaving her husband Cliff to carry the burden of grief alone.

D Supt Vinson, believed that Claire's killer was a local person and that he was being shielded by someone. This was reinforced by press speculation which was at times wildly inaccurate. Police had revealed that Ash-Smith had been questioned about the murder of Claire. This was no secret and happened after the attack on Charlotte Barnard in October 1995. Press reports now circulated that Ash-Smith had been detained and questioned soon after Claire's murder, but that his mother Diane had provided an alibi. This is just not true. Ash-Smith was not even considered to be a suspect for Claire's murder, let alone detained until nearly three years later, after he was arrested for the attack on Charlotte Barnard.

This false report was followed by renewed police interest in the Tiltman case, in particular, how the Criminal Justice Act 2003 (above) might be used in a fresh attempt to charge Colin Ash-Smith with the murder of Claire. In 2012, police were driven into making a decision as to whether to invoke the provisions of the 2003 Act concerning bad character evidence as they realised Ash-Smith, having served 16 years of his sentence, was due for a parole hearing and might be released. Whilst in prison he had been a model prisoner and had fully admitted the offences for

8. Originally a DCI, Vinson was promoted during the case so I use his higher rank throughout.

which he had been sentenced in 1996. There would be no valid reason not to release him on license.

In conjunction with the Crown Prosecution Service, the police decided to move against Ash-Smith and began to prepare their case against him. In order to use bad character evidence it is necessary for that evidence to be backed up and reinforced by other evidence. Bad character evidence on its own is insufficient. D Supt Vinson and his team took a serious look at what evidence was available to them.

They certainly had a likely suspect. Someone who had admitted attacking two other defenceless women within the small bounds of a Kentish town, both of which offences involved knives and stabbing. The offences were situated either side of the Tiltman murder creating what could be deemed a pattern. An experienced pathologist, Dr Heath had given his opinion that the assailant of Claire Tiltman was left-handed, reducing the pool of suspects to between 8% and 10% of the general population, and Ash-Smith was left-handed. As already described, enquiries had been made at the prisons where Ash-Smith had been serving his sentence and fellow prisoner Stefan Dubois gave evidence that Ash-Smith had told him he had attacked one of his victims near a zebra crossing (there was a zebra crossing at the top of London Road near the Esso filling station). Unfortunately for the prosecution, Dubois was adamant Ash-Smith had never ever told him he had killed Claire.

In September 2013 a police search of the Ash-Smith address in Dartford was carried out and a large quantity of Colin's clothing was seized. The search included the garden of the house and an allotment used by Aubrey Ash-Smith. The police were particularly interested in Colin's jacket which had been seized and tested when he was originally arrested in 1995 then subsequently returned with most of Colin's other belongings to the family after his trial. The jacket, together with a large quantity of his other clothes had long since been disposed of by the Ash-Smiths. However, the fact that police were frustrated in not having the jacket available to them for re-submission was greeted with some suspicion as to why the Ash-Smiths had disposed of it. Rational thought might have brought them to ask the question as to why anyone would hang on to old clothing of their children for 18 years. Aubrey Ash-Smith was quoted as saying, 'If I thought my son had killed Claire, I would disown him. But I believe he didn't do it.'

Also, in 2013, a documentary was presented by Professor David Wilson, Professor Emeritus of Criminology at Birmingham City University, for Channel 5 TV called *Killers Behind Bars*. It looked at various unsolved cases of murder in an attempt to throw light on the possible guilty parties by the use of a scientific approach of matching offences and their methodology to known serial killers currently in prison for similar offences. Not unlike the National Crime Faculty's efforts which had begun in 1995 with Operation Enigma, although with rather a lot more reliance on media-style headlining.

Operation Enigma looked at over 200 unsolved murders of females throughout the UK and applied computerised technology to establish links between them. These links included common factors such as the:

- type of injury;
- extent and number of injuries;
- victimology;
- geographic locations; and
- post mortem reports.

These factors were then sifted and combined to establish if there was a possibility that one person was responsible for one or more murders and whether there was sufficient correlation to justify a review. The enquiry found 21 possible clusters of two or more murders within the 200 plus cases. Amongst the groupings, in 1996 Operation Enigma came up with the startling theory that the Rachel Nickell, Samantha and Jazmine Bisset *and* the Claire Tiltman murders were linked by 'crime scene signatures'. As I say, this was in 1996: a time when 'confirmation bias' still declared that, despite his recent acquittal, Colin Stagg had murdered Rachel Nickell just as Colin Ash-Smith had murdered Claire Tiltman. One thing they could be sure of by 1996 is that Robert Napper had definitely murdered Samantha and Jazmine Bisset.

The *Killers Behind Bars* documentary hypothesis floated the notion that the person responsible for the murder of Claire was Robert Napper.

This flew in the face of the ingrained theory that Ash-Smith was responsible. Kent Police declined an invitation to appear on the programme. The reason given to Professor David Wilson for this non-participation was that they (Kent Police) did not want to narrow the search to just one person. Quite a rejection when compared to the efforts they were making to find evidence against Ash-Smith.

A guest on the same programme was ex-police officer Vincent Wright who had followed the Tiltman enquiry for many years in an amateur capacity. He also believed that Robert Napper could have murdered Claire. He pointed out to Professor Wilson the similarities to the other Napper murders and the description given by witnesses who had been in the area of the Tiltman murder describing a white male of 5' 8" to 5' 10" with brown hair and wearing white training boots. Napper had worn *white* Adidas training boots at the Bisset murders. Vincent had written to Kent Police as early as 2000 with his concerns and received a reply that Napper was serving a term of imprisonment when Claire was murdered on 18 January 1993. He wrote back to point out Napper had in fact been released early from prison on the last week of December 1992, three weeks before Claire's murder.

Vincent became aware that Kent Police were hot on the trail of Colin Ash-Smith and were about to charge him with murder. This was the very reason he tried to persuade the investigating team to seriously consider Napper as a possible suspect, with as much, if not more, 'circumstantial evidence' against him than Ash-Smith. Again, as in the Rachel Nickell enquiry, when confronted with the possibility of Napper being responsible, the investigators were not to be sidetracked from their goal of charging and convicting Ash-Smith. Just like in the Nickell investigation, when an alternative suspect was propped up it happened (for them) at the worse possible moment. They chose not to consider Napper as a credible suspect, not because he wasn't credible, but because they didn't want to derail their current conviction that Ash-Smith was their man.

In the meantime, in 2012 and as explained earlier in this book, Cliff Tiltman, Claire's father, also died. Both Claire's parents went to their graves carrying an unsatisfactory conclusion as to who had murdered their daughter. Although both were convinced Ash-Smith was responsible even though he had not yet been charged or convicted at this time.

By January 2014, rumours were starting to appear in the national press that DNA evidence had been found in a 'forensic breakthrough' on clothing discovered recently. This DNA evidence gave the police a 'copper bottomed case'. The case file, including the DNA evidence retrieved from an 'untouched bag of clothes' had been passed to the CPS and a suspect would be charged with Claire Tiltman's murder. Unfortunately, time proved the rumours not to be true. There was still no forensic evidence to support a charge against Ash-Smith.

Meanwhile in Walton Prison the date of Ash-Smith's parole board hearing had been set for 11 February 2014 and Diane and Aubrey Ash-Smith travelled to the prison hoping for good news. Their hopes were soon dashed as it was revealed by fax that on the very day of Colin's parole board he was to be charged with Claire's murder. On 12 February 2014 the press release was updated to: 'Man 45 to be charged over 1993 murder of 16-year-old Claire Tiltman after cold case review turns up DNA evidence'. That man was Colin Ash-Smith. Just what the breakthrough DNA evidence was remains a mystery. Certainly, no such evidence was produced at the forthcoming trial.

Now, the police and CPS had to present their case to a judge whose role was to decide whether there were grounds to support the use of evidence of bad character in any forthcoming trial. The heat was on prosecutors to convict Ash-Smith of the murder of Claire 21 years before. The first hurdle was this hearing to test the evidence. The hoped-for DNA evidence had not materialised. The confessional evidence from fellow prisoner Stefan Dubois was less than weak and could easily be exposed as such by any competent counsel. Nevertheless, the facts were put before Mr Justice Sweeney at Inner London Crown Court who was asked whether the case should be proceeded with and evidence of bad character allowed to be put forward during the trial. This bad character evidence would directly refer to and detail Ash-Smith's convictions for his knife wielding assaults on two defenceless women. After two days of deliberation the judge decided in the favour of the prosecution. The way was now clear for Colin's trial for the murder of Claire Tiltman to proceed. The prosecution team were delighted. Now they could introduce his previous convictions. Their case, based on circumstantial evidence, appeared to have been strengthened considerably.

CHAPTER 17

The BBC, the CPS and the Trial

'He is no lawyer who cannot take two sides.'— Charles Lamb (1775–1834)

By 2014 the fly-on-the-wall-type documentary had become commonplace. The BBC cast its net for something a little different and alighted on the premise of filming the Crown Prosecution Service (CPS) in action. To this end, they sent out film crews to CPS offices around the country. One of these happened to be in Maidstone, Kent, where they decided to feature preparations for the forthcoming trial of Colin Ash-Smith which was scheduled for hearing at Inner London Crown Court in November 2014.

This documentary entitled *The Prosecutors* is important as it illustrates what I believe to be a continuation of the same kind of confirmation bias I described in the preceding chapter. I can only invite readers to consider, from words spoken in the programme, the mindset of prosecutors and how this remained fixed from the moment they decided to allow police to charge Ash-Smith with Claire's murder right up to the trial's conclusion.[9]

The lead real life 'character' chosen by the programme makers was Nigel Pilkington, senior lawyer for CPS London south east. He was introduced and outlined the difficulties encountered by the prosecution, summarised the case and the key change in the law of evidence under the Criminal Justice Act 2003 allowing the use of evidence of bad character.

The current police SIO, D Supt Rob Vinson was also introduced. He gave a brief summary of the Charlotte Barnard attack. Then a photograph

9. The programme was not broadcast until after the trial so as not to prejudice its outcome. By the time it was shown Ash-Smith's conviction must have seemed to justify much of the content.

of Ash-Smith clothed in a police issue forensic jumpsuit was shown on screen. This was followed by a short video clip of Ash-Smith confessing to the attack on Charlotte during a police interview. No punches were pulled as viewers were immediately put in the picture as to his alleged bad character:

Question: 'Did you stab Charlotte Barnard with a knife?'

Ash-Smith: 'Yes I did.'

Q: 'Why did you do it?'

Ash-Smith: 'I don't know. It's on impulse. Most of the time I snap out of it.'

There were certainly no doubts left by the end of this short interview sample that Ash-Smith would fail the bad character test by a considerable margin. But in fairness, it was then pointed out that Ash-Smith categorically denied murdering Claire and that not one of the witnesses who had seen an unidentified male in the vicinity of the murder had subsequently picked him out at an identity parade. So far so fair. In the interests of complete fairness I should emphasise a few points concerning what I am about to say:

- Everything I write is directed towards a system in which, as an experienced investigator and reviewer of serious criminal cases, I have observed the risk of 'confirmation bias' (as outlined in earlier chapters). It is not a criticism of any individual practitioners involved. I write of an everyday phenomenon and potential cause of error against which justice must always guard.

- It is legitimate, I believe, to point out where in my view the facts as I have described them in other chapters of this book depart from those suggested during the programme (or trial) (that might have left viewers (or jurors) believing assertions were 'rock solid'). I have stayed close to the words used in the programme comparing these with the known evidence. Throughout, I invite readers to draw their own conclusions.

- I should caution readers that lawyers sometimes speak as if their version of events is 'fact' knowing that those *within the system* will understand that what they really mean is that this is what they assert subject to challenge by 'the other side'. Typically in the programme the words, 'I suggest', 'We suppose', 'We will try to show' and 'It is for others to judge' prefix much of what those seeking to establish Ash-Smith's guilt had to say.

- At the very start of the broadcast it was made clear that the CPS would be presenting *its* version of the facts based on the circumstantial evidence it planned to rely on in an attempt to prove the murder charge beyond reasonable doubt to the jury. Viewers were informed that a decision had to be made about which route the prosecution would take, focusing on evidence in support of its case. It is my contention that vital opposing strands of evidence were then ignored or allowed insufficient weight.

The cameras followed a meeting of CPS lawyers discussing the case one of whom thoughtfully proffered, 'So, the attacks stopped after Colin Ash-Smith was arrested.' Yes, they did. There is no doubt Ash-Smith attacked Beverley and Charlotte and that this type of attack ceased after his arrest. But this is not the question to be addressed. The similarities in the cases meant quite rightly that he remained a suspect in the Tiltman case, but were the dissimilarities given their proper due?

To introduce bad character evidence in court it has to amount to behaviour which is very similar to that in the offence for which the accused is currently on trial. Most importantly the prosecution can only rely upon it *as part* of its case. Prosecutors must persuade a judge and jury it isn't the only thing the accusation relies upon. There must be sufficient other evidence. It was this second part which seemed to be causing the prosecution most difficulty.

Not to be deterred and conscious of the admittedly 'high hurdle' facing prosecutors and that, by comparison, 'All the defence has to do is pick at things', CPS lawyer Nigel Pilkington explained, 'There is no point in doing this job unless you do difficult cases.' A noble sentiment, and a fine attitude, reinforced by an expectation that evidence would hopefully emerge to place Ash-Smith or his car close by. But, how to react if it didn't? As I will point out, several strands of the prosecution case were never confirmed by evidence, including where it was initially stated that it was hoped this would happen 'sooner or later'.

The cameras followed the CPS on a visit to the crime scene. This began at Claire Tiltman's home in Woodward Terrace and moved up to the top of London Road. Here Pilkington pondered aloud where the 14 minutes went from the time Claire was seen by the witness Lee Hooper to when she was murdered. He focused in on the packet of cigarettes with one missing, leading to the conclusion that Claire went to the corner shop in London Road to buy them. This is a credible theory, but cannot be verified. However, if Claire did go to the corner shop it would fit in neatly with the next part of the CPS theory which concerned a zebra crossing.

There is no actual evidence that Claire visited either the corner shop or the Esso garage (situated a little further up London Road past the zebra crossing), or other outlets. This the CPS acknowledged at one stage (as it did other problems with the evidence) making clear that it was no more than an assumption. The corner shopkeeper could not remember Claire visiting the shop that evening. Without corroboration it is pure supposition that she bought her cigarettes from one of these places. The woman who was on the Esso garage till that evening, Amanda Foster knew Claire by sight having seen her in the British Legion Club (but she did not know Colin Ash-Smith). Oddly there does not appear to be a statement from this witness in the police files.

There are statements from two other Esso employees, Sandra McGarry and Sharon Hewitt, neither of whom knew Claire, but both did know Colin Ash-Smith fairly well. After Ash-Smith was arrested for the Charlotte Barnard assault, they informed the police that Colin often parked his white Capri on the garage forecourt when visiting the British Legion Club. The Legion car-park in those days was clearly visible from the Esso cashier's counter. In any event neither of these two ladies were on duty at the Esso garage at the time of Claire's murder. It was they who informed police that the person on duty at 6 pm on the night of the murder was Amanda Foster.

When the till receipts were studied there was no record of the sale of ten cigarettes. The facts point to the conclusion that Claire did not visit the Esso garage. A friend of Claire's, Lisa Younger, said in her statement that she and Claire bought their cigarettes in the corner shop and not the Esso garage. If anyone knew about Claire's habits it was Lisa Younger. At this time in their lives they were very close friends. Many in their peer group called them 'Tilt and Milt' as they were so often seen together. Whatever their normal practice there was also no till receipt in the corner shop to verify the sale of ten cigarettes. The corner shopkeeper, who knew Claire by sight, said she had not visited his shop that evening. Yet the supposition that Claire had bought cigarettes in one of these two places seems to have taken hold in the TV representation of events.

It is curious that Amanda Foster (above) (who, as I say, knew Claire by sight), does not appear to have made a statement as she could possibly have finally cleared up whether Claire visited the Esso garage that evening. Any theory that ignores this 'evidential void' is I think further undermined by known witness sightings pointing to the conclusion that Claire could not have visited either place within the timeframe: see *Chapter 18*.

The 'zebra crossing' is of equally dubious relevance as I explained in *Chapter 16*. It is in London Road between the Esso garage and the nearby corner shop (see map). Ash-Smith in his witness statement made to police shortly after the murder in January 1993 claims he saw an unidentified person near to this crossing on the left pavement looking down London Road. This person Ash-Smith placed 'just before the crossing' as he drove past. Much later, his fellow prisoner Stefan Dubois made a statement in prison saying that Ash-Smith had told him he had attacked a girl near a zebra crossing (not 'killed' remember, or when or who).

It seems to have been important to the CPS that Ash-Smith was at this zebra crossing, where they argued that he saw Claire and followed her down London Road to the alleyway where he attacked her. Hence Pilkington musing to colleagues, 'He sees Claire on the zebra crossing. The zebra crossing is really important in this case... His [Ash-Smith's] plan is hatched in ten seconds. He is going to get in front of her. Kill her. Go round and double back to get his car.'

Other than Dubois' highly questionable evidence, references to Ash-Smith being on the (or any) zebra crossing are supported by no witness sightings at all. So it must be re-emphasised that this is theorising for the viewer, in line with the prosecution's version of events that they intended to convince the jury of in court. Hence also, e.g. 'A male is seen walking on the footpath. Described as 5' 8" to 5' 10". Twenty to 22 years, fair blond hair wearing a light-coloured full-length jacket. That is Colin Ash-Smith' and 'The more you look at it and the more you put your case together, Colin Ash-Smith did kill Claire Tiltman. That is the reality.' Reality seems a strong word to use when matters remained so questionable.

The first of the preceding quotes appears to be a reference to the evidence of the witness Kathleen Still, who actually gives the age as 25 to 26 years. At 6.12 pm, she saw a suspect in London Road whom she described as being on the side of the busy road without a pavement. This man was 5' 9" (sic not 5' 8") to 5' 10" and 25 to 26 years old, wearing a beige-coloured jacket. The man appeared to be talking to himself and had a 'baby face' (both incidentally traits of Robert Napper). Kathleen Still however failed to pick out Ash-Smith in a subsequent identity parade. So, this seems a rather certain version of events without anything tangible to back it up (other, it seems, than confirmation bias and the wish that another witness might come forward to join up the dots).

This thread of reasoning continued: 'The witness, French, walking from the station at 18.13 sees Claire walking with a man in front of her' and 'Mrs [Christine] Doyle from her window in Riverview sees a man aged about 40 with fair hair, the description of Colin Ash-Smith.' The discrepancy between ages 22 and 40 is stark. What appears to be happening here is that the CPS version conflates the two sightings as both being of Ash-Smith. Christine Doyle did not describe her sighting as having 'fair hair'. She clearly states she could not recall his hair colour (in fact later in the investigation the prosecution veer away from the value of her sighting).

Whoever the person Mrs Doyle saw in Ivy Bower Close was, that person was very unlike Colin Ash-Smith by her description. Furthermore, although she offered, she was not asked to attend any of the subsequent identity parades featuring him. This begs the question, if police and prosecutors thought that the person Mrs Doyle saw was Colin Ash-Smith, why was she not asked to attend an identity parade?

The CPS theory was then allowed to develop further on camera. 'His car, remember is at the top of the hill.' This it seems was intended to intimate that the suspect went up the alleyway into Riverview Road and then looped around back up the hill to collect his car. Nigel Pilkington's companions seem to accept this deduction, and at no stage contradict or question it. But it is not supported by actual evidence. He then touches on 'the three boys' who had seen a 'fast-walking man' near Greenhithe Railway Station just after the incident (see *Chapter 6*). He is asked directly by one of his colleagues, 'Are we using them?' and replies, 'No. Because they saw him go up an alley towards Stone Crossing Station.'

Similarly, references to a 'limping man' are rejected as being possibly because Ash-Smith injured himself in the attack (whereas I would argue that there is no such evidence of him being injured and secondly that this points to the way Robert Napper routinely walked, i.e. with a pronounced stoop and a loping gait). In fact, the three boys at the station saw a man answering the same description given by Christine Doyle in Ivy Bower Close immediately after the incident, hurrying away through an alleyway towards Stone Crossing Railway Station (the perfect place for an anonymous getaway on the train back to Plumstead). Not 'looping back'. But this evidence did not fit with the CPS theory that Ash-Smith, after killing Claire, doubled back to his car, via Eagles Road, at the top of London Road, in completely the opposite direction (see map).

It must be noted that Stone Crossing Railway Station is only a half mile walk from Greenhithe Railway Station. It is on the same train line and would have provided the man seen by Mrs Doyle and the three boys with a direct lift back to south east London. Something apparently deemed irrelevant by the CPS. By now, viewers of the BBC programme may have been thinking these assertions (which I would certainly challenge for the reasons I have given) were becoming 'rock solid'.

In fact, there are no witnesses whatsoever to say a car of the description of Ash-Smith's very distinctive white Ford Capri was hurriedly parked at the top of (or anywhere in) London Road at around the time of the murder. The descriptions given of the male seen heading towards Stone

Crossing were not followed up and did not form part of the identity parades that were subsequently held in which Ash-Smith featured.

In the programme, the CPS team continued their tour by following the trail from Riverview down to Greenhithe Railway Station. As they moved further from the crime scene, Pilkingon remarked, 'His car, remember, is at the top of the hill' (This as I have explained is conjecture and does not appear to tally with the accounts of any known witnesses). Furthermore, the next and nearby station at Stone Crossing was unmanned with no ticket office and at that time of evening would have been deserted on the 'up' line to London.

Continuing with the BBC documentary, the presenter explained how Ash-Smith had completed 17 years of his life sentence and applied for parole. The parole hearing was now postponed until after his trial for the murder of Claire. With five and half weeks to go before the trial a case conference was held in the chambers of Brian Altman QC who explained the roles of prosecuting and defence counsel. He would be acting for the prosecution and set out how he would tie all the admittedly circumstantial evidence together to present a case and 'persuade' the jury.

Nigel Pilkington offered his thoughts on the 'bad character' evidence: 'We say in four separate cases he always gives a false alibi. This alone shows evidence of bad character' (There were as far as I can tell only two existing cases, Godfrey and Barnard and no evidence of false alibis, since Ash-Smith promptly admitted to both those offences). He then referred directly to Colin Ash-Smith's voluntary report made the day after the murder as 'setting up his alibi' elaborating, 'This is what he always does. He gets in early. He makes a big mistake. He says 6.30 pm. That's just not the right time.' Then, 'Six days later in his statement he changes it.'

I must agree this is a fair point. Ash-Smith did alter the time from his first report, from 6.30 pm (Claire was murdered at approximately 6.20 pm) to saying in his statement to police he was at home with his parents after the delivery of a letter to Ted Wells at 6 pm. Ash-Smith could have realised his mistake, but would he have known the exact time of Claire's death to the minute? Could this discrepancy have been made innocently? Just as many other timings provided by members of the public in the immediate aftermath were approximations (see further

Chapter 18). Certainly, it gave no cause for suspicion to police investigators at the time. If the explanation is that Ash-Smith was actually telling the truth, and there is no evidence he was not (see later), where is the evidence of him lying?

The documentary continued to focus more and more on the CPS position for the forthcoming trial and they appeared to be convinced that they could obtain a conviction. However, talking straight to camera, Pilkington candidly announced, 'Some will look at this case and say, "I don't know what you are doing Nigel. You haven't got a case here."' It is not clear who this statement refers to. His own colleagues, his peers, other CPS decision-makers, or people like myself who have studied and assessed the facts differently. At the very least, some cognitive dissonance seems to have existed. 'Jeopardy', I think programme makers like to call it. I believe this further underlines the uncertainty that appeared to exist in the minds of both police and prosecutors right to the very end of this case (and documentary) about whether they could secure a conviction. That is until the jury brought in its verdict of guilty.

Anyone who sees the film cannot help but feel the sense of relief that flowed from the jury's guilty verdict and that, until then, things were indeed 'on a knife edge'. This was never, ever an open or shut case. Indeed, Pilkington, to be fair, had already commented to camera, 'It is circumstantial with no direct evidence', although I have to disagree with the rider he then added: 'And yet the case is overwhelming.' How could it be?

A final look towards the camera and, 'At the end of the day it's just about judgement.' With which I wholeheartedly agree. That judgement would of course fall to the jury after hearing all the evidence not just those things alleged from a CPS standpoint.

So convinced did the CPS seem to be that a witness would come forward to assist their case that Pilkington at one point declared, 'Sooner or later someone will see Colin Ash-Smith near Knockhall Chase.' A wish which would conveniently place Ash-Smith at the right time in the right place to give him the opportunity to kill Claire and confirm the CPS version of events. Yet this hoped-for witness has never, ever materialised. Rather than someone coming forward to identify a well-known local man in a very distinctive car, could it possibly be that Ash-Smith was never out of his Ford Capri in London Road at the relevant time and his car was never hurriedly parked near Knockhall Chase? This possibility was studiously shunned by prosecution lawyers and investigators alike.

Even some of the witnesses the prosecution did possess are looked at in what seems to be a rather peculiar manner by some of those in the programme. The evidence of Danny French who saw a male at 6.15 pm walking closely in front of Claire in London Road is viewed as 'a disappointment': 'A different description of the jacket which is disappointing because we don't think Colin Ash-Smith was wearing such a jacket.' But on what basis? Danny French described the clothing in question as, 'A waist-length, light-coloured jacket.' Ash-Smith did own a vaguely similar jacket and he wore it at Claire's funeral. He was photographed wearing it, but this raised no police suspicions at the time. The jacket, along with other items of his clothing was submitted for forensic testing and came back negative as to any contact with or trace of Claire. It was then returned to Colin's parents.

As explained in *Chaper 16*, when the murder was re-investigated in 2013, the police searched Diane and Aubrey's home again and seized more of Colin's clothing. They were disappointed to discover that the Ash-Smiths had disposed of much of it, including the jacket which they had hoped to re-submit for testing. With a lapse of 18 years, it is hardly suspicious for them to have disposed of their son's old clothes.

It was at this point whilst the documentary was being made that submissions were heard at Inner London Crown Court and the case was given the go ahead to proceed to trial. Diane and Aubrey Ash-Smith were at court to hear this news and see their son, who until recently had been hopeful of release after his parole board hearing, sent back to prison to await his trial. All plans of parole were shelved, or at least put on hold to await his trial for the murder of Claire Tiltman.

Again as earlier described, the Crown Court hearing before Mr Justice Sweeney for him to determine whether there was sufficient evidence to support a prosecution lasted for two days. The central point under discussion was whether evidence of bad character could be levied against Ash-Smith. Without it the chances of a successful prosecution (despite the confidence of the CPS team) remained slim. They, along with SIO

D Supt Vinson were jubilant when the judge, after long deliberation, concluded that the bad character evidence would be admissible.

The BBC documentary continued to cover the proceedings up to the trial. Now a focus was placed upon prosecuting counsel, Brian Altman, a member of Queen's Counsel (QC),[10] who was interviewed in his chambers. A highly respected lawyer with a record that includes appearing in many high-profile cases, he explained how he used, 'devices' to 'impress' a jury: 'My job as an advocate is to persuade. If I cannot persuade on the basis of the opening, I'm not doing my job.'

For legal reasons, the cameras could not follow proceedings in the courtroom where, over a trial lasting four weeks, 19 live witnesses were presented by and for the prosecution. The evidence of a further 88 witnesses was read to the court. This is common practice where the evidence is uncontested and can cover all sorts of mundane facts, which however are still required to be given in evidence.

It was with eager anticipation that Stefan Dubois was called to the witness stand. D Supt Vinson had already revealed his misgivings over the evidence of Dubois who was to assert that Ash-Smith had confessed to him whilst in prison that he had murdered Claire. Despite hopes for other, similar cell confessions, this source had proved particularly barren as noted in *Chapter 16*. Dubois was a close friend of Ash-Smith and, unusually, this friendship continued long after Dubois had been released from custody. Altman described him as a 'key witness'. Vinson was rather more circumspect describing what was revealed as, 'Not a straightforward confession' and in one of the quieter asides in the BBC programme was heard to comment that even if Ash-Smith did mention an attack on a zebra crossing this may have been 'bravado'.

To recap, Ash-Smith had been told whilst he was prison, by his solicitor, Nadir Prabatani, that Dubois was giving evidence against him. Ash-Smith then telephoned Dubois to clarify what exactly was being said. Dubois told him of police interest in the story around Ash-Smith being in the vicinity of a zebra crossing at the time of Claire's murder. They would have both been aware that such telephone calls are routinely

10. Now King's Counsel or KC.

recorded, as indeed this one was. Ash-Smith was heard referring to the police interest in the zebra crossing in a light-hearted vein. He appeared not in the least perturbed or angry with Dubois and told him, 'It's quite comical. It is a serious thing, but there is nothing there that relates to this offence' (Claire's murder).

Despite any reservations, D Supt Vinson took a different view, stating, 'We mention it because it is extremely relevant to what happened on that day. It fits into what the case is and that is what makes it so powerful.' Vinson like the others was clearly convinced that mention of the zebra crossing had important relevance, but no-one ever seemed clear about what that relevance was. This is especially odd as Ash-Smith himself is recorded in his first witness statement saying that he drove past the zebra crossing in his Ford Capri. That is all and the police thought nothing of this.

In the witness box Dubois was asked by defence barrister David Nathan QC, 'Tell me the context about which Colin spoke about the zebra crossing.' To which Dubois replied, 'I have no idea. I was on medication. I have gaps.' Hardly the cell confession trumpeted by the prosecution. In short, Ash-Smith never confessed to anyone in prison, cellmate or otherwise, that he had murdered Claire. Quite the opposite, he had consistently denied killing Claire to anyone and everyone who would listen.

The trial continued as a rather one-sided affair. In the documentary, Brian Altman QC took a rather direct view of the objectives of Ash-Smith's defence team: 'Part of the defence is to pin their colours to other individuals. One of whom was a serial killer.' This was a reference to none other than Robert Napper, who as Altman predicted was put forward by the defence as an alternative suspect. But this was somewhat watered down by them also including the possibility of Peter Rivers being the culprit and reference was made to Rivers' suicide note in which, as described in *Chapters 3* and *12*, he seemed to have obliquely 'confessed' to the Tiltman murder. All of this gave the appearance of a 'shopping list' or 'fishing exercise' on the part of the defence that seems to have lacked the force of the arguments I make in this book pointing towards Napper specifically.

In the defence opening speech a direct reference was made to Napper and a photograph taken of him in 1994 was shown to the jury to study. This was the photograph taken by the Bisset enquiry surveillance team near Napper's address in Plumstead High Street in which he is wearing the hip-length tan-coloured coat.[11] Nathan pointed out, 'This is the face of Robert Napper taken in 1994.' He continued, 'In a few months either side of the killing of Claire Tiltman, he [Napper] killed at least three people. He lived in Plumstead. It is a very short train ride to Greenhithe. That may be significant.' Indeed, it may well be significant. However, nothing further was made of this suggestion. None of the witnesses who had made statements describing a man who may have been Napper were called to give evidence and they remained on the 'unused witness' list. Altman summed up the defence line of attack perfectly, 'The difference between us [prosecution and defence] is I have to prove it was his client. He [David Nathan QC] doesn't have to prove it was either of the other two.' This is a perfect statement of the 'Golden Thread' of English criminal law which holds that this burden is always on the prosecutor and that the accompanying standard of proof which he or she must discharge is beyond reasonable doubt.[12] But I would ask whether anyone could convict beyond reasonable doubt on such debatable evidence?

On day 15 of the trial the defence decided to call Ash-Smith to give his own evidence. The news of this was greeted with uncontained glee from the prosecution camp. It is not necessary for the defendant to take to the stand to give his own version of events but Colin Ash-Smith, guided by his defence team, decided to do so. If Altman thought Ash-Smith would crack under his cross-examination he was wrong. It became rather a rhetorical list of accusation followed by firm rebuttals and categorical denials such as 'I know I didn't kill Claire.' Another example of this: Altman: 'You don't have an alibi at all. It's all made up and invented. Isn't it?' to which Ash-Smith simply replied, 'No.'

Altman still firmly argued that the zebra crossing in London Road was the key to it all. When talking to a group of Claire's old school friends in his chambers during a break in proceedings, he told them, 'There's a

11. See the image on page 184.
12. There are limited exceptions to this Golden Thread none of which arise here.

beautiful thread running through. It's the zebra crossing.' He also added, rather poignantly, but maybe prophetically, 'And I hope history doesn't say I'm wrong.'

Throughout the trial Diane and Aubrey Ash-Smith had been treated disgracefully by some of Claire's supporters and had not been able to take their places in court to watch the trial. Most of the venom directed towards them was from third party members of the public who had no direct knowledge of the case and had made up their own minds that not only was Colin Ash-Smith guilty but also that his parents were liars and trying to shield their son from justice. At the previous hearing at The Old Bailey, boyfriends of the now adult schoolgirl friends of Claire shouted abuse from the public gallery towards them.

As the trial drew to its conclusion it was decided by the defence team not to call Diane Ash-Smith as an alibi witness. She was told by the defence team that her evidence was tainted, and she would be 'ripped to shreds' in the witness box. Taking a step back, it is true Diane had been charged with attempting to pervert the course of justice in encouraging her husband Aubrey to destroy one of Colin's knives. However, she was found not guilty of that offence. She was an experienced politician and well-used to public speaking. She was willing to swear on oath that Colin had been with her all of the evening of 18 January 1993 with the exception of when she briefly delivered a letter to Ted Wells. A distance of only four yards and never out of sight. The tragedy was that by not giving evidence of alibi (whatever the risks), Colin was left high and dry. All members of the jury must have wondered whether, if Colin was to be believed when he had said he was at home with his mother at the relevant time, then where was she and why didn't she alibi him on oath?

It is understandable why Aubrey wasn't called to give alibi evidence for his son. He'd been convicted of attempting to pervert the course of justice. He would have faced a torrid time in the witness box. But even his tainted evidence was preferable to the guilt induced silence. It is also peculiar that the evidence of Dr Michael Heath was accepted by the defence without any challenge to ask how he came to the conclusion the assailant was left-handed nearly three years after the event. I deal with this further in *Chapter 21*.

On the twenty-second day the closing speeches were made to the jury. Here it seems all the defence was left with was to base their submissions around what the jury must, by now, have been thinking was the rather tired assertion that 'someone else might have done it': 'The big question you (the jury) have to resolve is can you be sure that Colin Ash-Smith killed and murdered Claire Tiltman. Is there a realistic possibility that someone other than Ash-Smith killed Claire?' David Nathan QC continued in this vein until, finally, turning to the jury he said, 'This is all guesswork on the part of the prosecution. How can that be a safe basis to find anyone guilty of murder?'

Nathan's last comment hit the nail on the head. But it was too late, and the point was made only after so many opportunities seem to have been lost during the course of the trial to underline just how unsafe the conviction of Ash-Smith would be. The jury were out for one day whilst they considered the matters before them. With a unanimous verdict they found Colin Ash-Smith guilty of the murder of Claire Tiltman.

The whole access to the prosecution lawyers (coupled with the outcome in Ash-Smith's case after all the uncertainty) was a coup for the BBC and the producers must have thought they had struck gold. But I might suggest that the media, driven by a need to both inform and entertain viewers, may not feel constrained by the same high standards as those criminal justice practitioners it persuades to become involved. Though *The Prosecutors* was edited with skill, this may also account for the way in which some of the more enticing 'soundbites' were presented.

Somc of those being 'followed' seem to have got off lightly and the opportunity to take the programme in a different, more critical, direction was missed. I can only question whether this amounted to a clouded attitude towards British Justice. Perhaps the programme put the lawyers and prosecutors under a new form of scrutiny. Maybe lawyers are often given the opportunity to pore over and examine the actions of others in luxurious hindsight, but not (certainly in those days) in the full glare of the TV cameras. To my mind the documentary's greatest achievement was to demonstrate questionable approaches and reasoning when set against the hard facts I have set out in this book.

The old Station Road under the railway at Greenhithe, looking towards what was the Railway Hotel. © Vincent Wright

The former Railway Hotel on the corner of London Road and Bean Road. The alley is just behind the traffic lights on the left. © Vincent Wright

CHAPTER 18

Do Not Get Confused by the Facts

'When a fact appears opposed to a long train of deductions it invariably proves to be capable of bearing some other interpretation.'— *The Valley of Fear*, Arthur Conan Doyle (1859–1930)

In this chapter I seek to demonstrate once and for all how the theory of Claire Tiltman being followed by her attacker from the top of London Road near the Esso garage and zebra crossing to where she met her end in the alleyway leading to Riverview Road just does not add up. As the reader follows the progress of Claire from her home in Woodward Terrace it would be helpful to cross-reference her journey with the maps reproduced at the start of this book.

On the evening of 18 January 1993, Claire was at home with her mother Linda Tiltman. A little after 6 pm, she left her house to visit a friend in Riverview Road, a journey which at a steady walking pace should take about 20 minutes. Her mother estimated that Claire exited the front door at 6.10 pm. This was, however, only a judgement made two days after the event in Linda's formal statement dated 20 January 1993 and she couldn't be certain of the exact time.

Claire is next seen by Stephen Tolfree, a neighbour who knew her by sight. Tolfree was returning from the Circle K shop (not to be confused with the Corner Shop in Knockhall Chase) when he almost bumped into Claire as they both turned the corner of London Road/Woodward Terrace. Tolfree stated he had left his home in Carlton Avenue near to Woodward Terrace at 6 pm and walked the 200 yards to the Circle K shop where he spent three to four minutes before returning home. His calculation of the time when he saw Claire was 6.05/6.06 pm (slightly earlier than Linda Tiltman's estimate). Two car drivers were driving independently along London Road towards Gravesend. Neither witness recognised Claire, but both gave a very good description and, with the absence of any other people walking alongside the road, the sightings were almost certainly of Claire. One of the drivers, Lisa Richards, saw this person on the north footpath at the junction with the entrance to Stone Place Road and London Road. It would appear Claire had crossed over to the north side of London Road using the pelican crossing nearly opposite the Circle K shop. Stone Place Road leads to Stone Crossing Railway Station. The other driver, Jacqueline Gower, saw what seems to have been the same young woman, still on the north footway, at the London Road junction with the lane leading to St Mary the Virgin church. Jacqueline also noticed a man behind Claire who appeared to be 'staring at her'. Both timed these sightings at approximately 6.10 pm.

The next sighting was further down London Road, this time on the south footway, so Claire must have re-crossed the road. The witness Lee Hooper knew Claire by name; they both attended the British Legion Karate Club. Hooper was on the north footway heading towards Dartford and 'nodded' to Claire across the road. He was unsure if she responded. The place where he saw Claire was next to a large field used for grazing horses. Hooper had left home at 5.54 pm. He could be fairly sure of the time because, as he left, his father was making a telephone call home from his place of work and this was timed by BT as ending at 5.54 pm. In a second statement, Lee Hooper said he left his house as the call was ending. A later police reconstruction of the walk timed it as 12 minutes from Lee Hooper's house to where he saw Claire. This would make the time of his sighting of Claire 6.06 pm at the latest.

All of the above witnesses describe Claire as walking 'normally' and not in any hurry. Hooper and Jacqueline Gower also describe a male figure walking in the same direction as Claire, behind her. This male was never identified during the subsequent massive investigation.

Raymond Hurt is the jogger mentioned in *Chapter 7*. He gave a very good description of a young woman he saw twice in London Road. The first time, as he jogged up the hill on the south footway towards Dartford, he saw her close to the Jacqueline Gower sighting, but Claire was now on (his) the south footway. He estimates the time then to have been 6.10 pm. Hurt collected a prescription, which was waiting for him at the Woodward Terrace surgery and without delay returned, jogging along the same route. He passed Claire again about 40 feet from the junction of London Road and Bean Road. She was still walking at a natural pace. He estimates the second sighting as 6.16/6.18 pm. Raymond Hurt has no recollection of a male person on the footway.

The next firm sighting was that of Danny French. French got off the London to Greenhithe train at 6.08 pm. He was the last passenger to alight from the train and then walked along Station Road, turned left into London Road and walked up the hill on the north footpath towards his home in Knockhall Chase. He passed the alleyway and began to fiddle with his Sony Walkman cassette player which needed a change of tape. He became aware of someone approaching and saw a young woman, who by his very good description appeared to be Claire. He stepped aside to allow her to pass as she continued walking down London Road towards the access to the alleyway. Interestingly, just before he passed Claire, he was passed by a man ahead of her, also heading down the hill on the north footway. Danny French's brief description of this man was white, clean shaven wearing a light-coloured jacket. A later timed reconstruction by the police of French's walk indicated French passed the alleyway at 6.15 pm, passed the white male at 6.17 pm and what appeared to be Claire at 6.19 pm. The re-timed walk continued up London Road to Knockhall Chase arriving at a position near the corner shop at 6.23 pm.

There were four witnesses who were in the vicinity who heard screams. Denise Spencer was at home in her house which backs onto the alleyway. She was watching TV and during the commercial break after 6.15 pm she heard two loud screams a few seconds apart followed by a series of short screams. Kelly Wales was inside the doctors' surgery in the waiting-room in Ivy Bower Close. At 6.20 pm, she heard two faint screams a few seconds apart. Four minutes later, at 6.24 pm the surgery receptionist came into the doctor's room and said a girl had been injured outside and there was a lot of blood. Mark Ingram and Angela Archer were in their car driving along London Road and, as they passed the alleyway, they both heard two short screams. They timed the screams as being at 6.20 pm.

Paul Harris and Gitte Hansen were in their car in London Road facing towards Gravesend waiting to turn right into Mounts Road. As they drove past the alleyway, they both saw Claire run out of it waving her arms and looking back up the alleyway. Gitte was closer and described the look on Claire's face as 'panic stricken'. Paul Harris looked in his rear-view mirror and saw Claire collapse against the low wall. The first message to the emergency services was made by Christine Bance, a customer in the Railway Hotel, after Ron Wilson had run into the pub calling out fore someone to phone for an ambulance. That call was logged by the telephone operator at 6.23 pm.

Two other witnesses came forward. Diane and Glen Eversfield were driving in London Road towards Dartford at the relevant time. They were in separate cars having just picked up their children from Diane's sister's house off Mounts Road. Glen Eversfield left first at between 6.15 and 6.20 pm. He drove along Mounts Road towards London Road. As he approached the junction to turn left into London Road he saw a male standing on the junction to his left facing the BT telephone exchange. The man seemed to be hesitating, waiting to cross the road. Glen described him as white, late-twenties about six feet tall. He could not describe him further and saw no-one else. He turned left into London Road and continued on his way.

His wife Diane followed on the same route only two minutes later in the second car. She turned left into London Road and saw what she described as a 'young lad' stagger as if drunk out of the alleyway. Diane looked into her rear view mirror and saw this 'young man' totter up the hill and collapse to 'his' knees by the low wall near the alleyway entrance. This 'young man' could only have been Claire. The fleeting description of the male at Mounts Road junction given by Glen Eversfield better resembles the description given by Christine Doyle than it does Colin Ash-Smith. The unidentified male was never traced.

A moment's supposition. Claire could have slipped into quiet Breakneck Hill to have a cigarette before resuming her journey to Riverview Road through the alleyway. Breakneck Hill is away from the eyes of commuters and eerily quiet. The unknown male, perhaps the same male seen behind her earlier in London Road, could have followed her into the alleyway where he attacked her. Certainly the timings of the Eversfields would support this theory. Furthermore Glen Eversfield saw the male about to cross the road from Mounts Road to the north footway of London Road. If Claire had been followed by Ash-Smith down London Road from Knockhall Chase, Ash-Smith would have been on the north footway of London Road as there is no footway on the south side. Who was the man Glen Eversfield saw moments before Claire was murdered?

It can be seen clearly from the timings given by witnesses that a fairly accurate picture of Claire's movements up to the time she was attacked can be built up. There are some minor discrepancies which leave a leeway of up to four minutes either way. Of what we can be absolutely certain is that the ambulance was called at 6.23 pm. This means all of the witness timings must have been before this. Upon examining the timings and the way in which Claire was walking (naturally and in no hurry) there is insufficient time within the above timeframe for her to have walked from the Bean Road junction straight up to the Knockhall Chase junction (a distance of 0.3 miles), up a steep hill, then buy cigarettes and return back down the hill to the alley entrance (0.2 miles). A total of 0.5 miles (0.8 kilometre).

The real mystery is: why was she was in London Road and east of the alleyway entrance? The obvious route to her friend's house in Riverview Road was left into Station Road and then right into Riverview Road: a route which was well lit and was the most direct. We will never know the answer to this and can only go forward on the information we have, which clearly puts Claire at one point near the Mounts Road/London Road junction. What we do know, however, is that some of the schoolchildren used this alley as a regular cut through. Indeed, Claire's friend, Vicky Swift, had walked through the same alley at about 5 pm that evening after getting off the school bus. The alley afforded a flatter route into Riverview Road, avoiding the hilly approach off Station Road. It was also a shortcut to the doctors' surgery in Ivy Bower Close.

The police took statements from witnesses who had seen Claire and timed their own walks to better assess and accurately estimate their times. I cannot find a record of them doing the same for Claire to see how her movements fitted in. With Vincent Wright I have done the walk from

Claire's house in Woodward Terrace at a steady pace to the alleyway. A distance of 0.8 miles (1.28 kilometres) which takes 15 minutes. The time of her attack was, taking all the information into account, between 6.15 pm and 6.20 pm. If she had carried on walking up the hill to the corner shop it would have taken her at least another five minutes, arriving at the corner shop/zebra crossing at 6.19 pm. The return walk downhill in London Road to the alleyway takes another four to five minutes. This would put her at the entrance to the alley at the earliest at 6.24 pm. Clearly this was after her attack, and after the first call to the ambulance service.

Once the times are laid out in this precise way it can be seen the intelligence on Claire's movements just prior to her attack is considerable. The prosecution theory of Claire being at the top of Knockhall Chase where they believe she was seen by Colin Ash-Smith on the zebra crossing, who then parks his distinctive car and after that follows her down London Road (*Chapter 17*), is not possible. That theory continues whereby the perpetrator is supposed to get ahead of her before the entrance to the alleyway, guesses she will follow him into the alley, kills her and then make his way via a circuitous route along Eagles Road back up to Knockhall Chase to pick up his car. When studied in conjunction with the facts set out in this chapter this theory is just not credible. The CPS, remember, were holding-out on this perceived scenario, convinced a witness would come forward who saw either Ash-Smith, or his car, near the vicinity of the zebra crossing at the top of London Road. Witnesses that never have and, I suggest, never will, materialise. For the simple reason that Colin Ash-Smith wasn't there. All this information was in the police system at the time of the investigation and a 'timeline' may have been drawn up to aid comprehension. I have found no reference to such a document.

One final point on the critical timing of witnesses who saw Claire. The question surrounding the packet of ten cigarettes with one cigarette missing has puzzled investigators. It was posited by the CPS that Claire visited the corner shop in Knockhall Chase to buy these (although there is no till receipt or witness to confirm this). The reason surmised for her trip to the shop is that its owner may have had a 'relaxed' attitude towards youngsters buying cigarettes. I remind readers, Claire had just had her sixteenth birthday and could now legally buy cigarettes. She strikes me as the type of character who would relish the opportunity of now being challenged over such an issue. Also consider this. There was one cigarette missing. Proof, some might say, she had just bought them. But, within the tight time frame? Making the trip up London Road to the corner shop in Knockhall Chase was only possible if she ran the whole way there and back. As I say above, it is a distance of approximately one mile. How then did she manage to run down the hill of London Road whilst smoking a cigarette?

Surveillance photo of Robert Napper, 1993. © Metropolitan Police

D Supt Owen Taylor holds a witness appeal poster featuring Claire's photograph headlined 'MURDER'. © PA Photos/Alamy

CHAPTER 19

Napper: Now You See Me, Now You Don't

In the view of the police, the CPS and the general population of Greenhithe a memorable victory had been scored. Justice had been seen to be done. At last, the running sore of just who had murdered Claire Tiltman had finally been resolved. Colin Ash-Smith had been convicted of her murder and sentenced to life imprisonment. The term 'life' in this case meant serving a minimum term of 21 years before parole might be considered. In the township of Greenhithe a feeling of a job well done was uppermost in peoples' minds. Aubrey and Diane Ash-Smith continued living in Stone and to receive unpleasant reminders of their son's guilt through unsolicited phone calls and terms of abuse shouted at them in the street from the more moronic section of the community. They still believed in their son Colin's innocence regarding the murder and were never shy of expressing their views on the matter. They fully accepted his guilt in the attacks on Charlotte Barnard and Beverley Godfrey but could never bring themselves to believe Colin had killed Claire. An unsurprising attitude if he was in the house with them at the time of her murder.

Press and media interest started to wane after the conviction. This wasn't surprising, after all the community almost without exception believed Ash-Smith was guilty, many of them having probably made up their minds before the trial. In any event it can never be denied that Colin Ash-Smith was a dangerous sex offender who without doubt had committed two appalling attacks on defenceless women. Apart from his mother and father who cared if he was in prison? The community were satisfied. A trial had been staged and a successful prosecution achieved. A murder which had puzzled repeated investigations since its commission in January 1993 and up to the trial in December 2014 had now been solved.

An appeal was entered in 2015 on the grounds that Mr Justice Sweeney had allowed into the trial 'gravely prejudicial evidence', a reference to the bad character evidence. It was rejected by Lord Justice Davis and two other Lords Justice of Appeal largely on the basis that nothing improper had taken place legally speaking. Surely, that was an end to it?

In the interim and prior to the trial both of Claire's parents had died. As also mentioned in earlier chapters, Aubrey Ash-Smith died, in April 2016, one year and a half after the trial. Enter onto the scene a member of the public who had taken a close interest in the high-profile case of Rachel Nickell. Vincent Wright had a short career as a police officer in the 1980s and left the Metropolitan Police in 1986 to pursue a lifelong ambition to travel around the world. This was initially intended to be a break of one or two years and then he would return to a police career. In fact, three years passed before he returned to the UK and instead of resuming his police service he was offered and took up a job as a Marine Seismic Observer in the offshore oil and gas industry. The new job suited him well and he left the police force for good.

The change of direction in his career did not deter his appetite for investigating crime. That interest was rekindled when, knowing he had a long period at sea coming up, and having taken an interest in the Rachel Nickell case, he bought Paul Britton's book *The Jigsaw Man* to take with him as reading material whilst working on *MV Labrador Horizon* out of Mobile, Alabama in the Gulf of Mexico. This is how in 1996, through reading that book, he became fascinated by the opinions of Britton, whilst at the same time a seed of doubt entered his mind telling him that Colin Stagg was not responsible for Rachel's murder.

On his return on leave to the UK, Vincent started to dig deeper into the case and to expand his research, which included site visits to Wimbledon, researching local newspapers and reading all other available material about the Nickell case. This included books by journalists and also one by the now retired detective inspector who was the deputy SIO on the Nickell case, DI Keith Pedder. Pedder left the Metropolitan Police after the Nickell case and subsequently, against serious opposition from the Metropolitan Police, published a book setting out his view of the investigation, entitled *The Rachel Files*, in 2001. This was just before the revelations by DNA evidence that Robert Napper had murdered her. (It is plain from reading Pedder's book that at that the time and before it was found otherwise he still believed Stagg was responsible).

By then, however, Vincent Wright was becoming more and more convinced that Napper, not Stagg was responsible. He started to compile a case file and felt so strongly about his suspicions that he contacted the Nickell investigating team at Wimbledon. It was arranged for him to meet a member of that team at Southampton Police Station in 1996. The detective sergeant listened to him, but it was painfully apparent she had no time for theories from members of the public. The meeting lasted barely 15 minutes and Vincent, in his own words, was made to feel like a 'nutter'. This setback dampened his enthusiasm towards sharing his research with the police investigators, although he quietly continued to gather all the information he could that was in the public domain.

In 1999, he felt he had added enough information to his file to consult the police again and a meeting was set up with DI Pedley (not to be confused with DI Pedder). In fact, I had contacted Pedley (then a detective sergeant) when we (the Bisset enquiry team) suggested Napper as a suspect back in 1995. I remember it well because it concerned the markings in Napper's *A to Z*. We thought we had discovered a mark made by Napper next to Wimbledon Windmill which is very close to the Nickell murder scene. The 'mark' turned out to be a printer's error and this gave them a convenient 'get out' clause to not investigate the matter further, whilst also reinforcing the Nickell team's view that other anomalies we had found were of dubious provenance and little worth.

The meeting between Vincent and DI Pedley went much better than the earlier contact he'd had with the investigating team in Southampton. He was received politely and listened to. By this time, he was armed with much more material. He had done an in-depth study of what Robert Napper was doing between the death of Rachel Nickell in July 1992 and the murders of Jazmine and Samantha Bisset in November 1993. However, although he was listened to and given a promise that all his research would be studied with a view to looking at Napper as a suspect, he never heard back from DI Pedley or anyone else on the Nickell team.

Vincent started to look at other murders which could fit the profile of Robert Napper. It must be remembered that he was working entirely alone at this point and continuing his dogged enquiries using local newspaper reports and libraries. He had built up an impressive file showing other murders that Napper might be considered for, including those of Debbie Linsley, Jean Bradley, Penny Bell and Patricia Parsons in addition to that of Claire Tiltman. But it was the Claire Tiltman case which really intrigued him.

By 1999, Vincent had changed jobs again and was now working for a construction firm in the Woolwich area of south east London. This gave him ample opportunity to pursue his pastime. He took to following the Green Chain routes used by Napper. His work extended out to Dartford and Greenhithe and he again took the chance to study more of the Claire Tiltman murder all the while building up a picture of her case. He was interested to find statements which were not in the court system and had been 'unused' at the trial. Particularly those of the three boys who saw a suspect just after the murder wearing white training boots and who had a strange walk, near Greenhithe Railway Station heading away from the scene towards Stone Crossing Railway Station. The same three witnesses that CPS lawyers in the BBC documentary explained that they had decided against calling to court to give evidence in favour of presenting the prosecution version of events described in *Chapter 17*.

In 2003, Vincent wrote to Commander Andre Baker of the Metropolitan Police and laid out the coincidences and commonalities of the murders of Rachel Nickell, the Bissets, Jean Bradley and Claire Tiltman. This was at the same time as the Metropolitan Police were conducting a cold case review into the unsolved murder of Rachel. A review, unbeknown to Vincent, that I had an input into.

By 2004, hopes were rising in the review team assigned to the Nickell case that there may be forensic evidence which might point to a suspect. Vincent received a letter from Commander Baker in which he expressed his thanks and a promise to forward all of his research to the review team. Vincent heard nothing more until he was contacted in 2005 by D Sgt

Ivan Agnew who wanted to discuss the matter (see below). An article had already appeared in the *Daily Mail* in November 2004 in which it was claimed Robert Napper was Nickell's killer. Vincent's suspicions were beginning to be vindicated.

In 2005, Vincent made his first direct approach to the Kent Police through DI Short. The reason for this was that he, Vincent, had found in the court records at Woolwich a document which showed that Napper had been released from his short prison sentence on 23 December 1992, some three weeks before the murder of Claire Tiltman. Vincent had already noted that Kent Police had written off Napper as a suspect because they believed he was in prison at the time of her murder. He felt obliged to apprise them of their error. He was again received politely and listened to but given no feedback and was not contacted by Kent Police again. As already noted, it was also in 2005 that Vincent was contacted out of the blue by D Sgt Agnew of the Metropolitan Police murder team who was a part of what was by then the re-investigation of the murder of Rachel Nickell.

D Sgt Agnew was very interested in the considerable research Vincent had done and it was with a sense of relief that he, Vincent, handed over all of this work (as he had to DI Pedley five years before) at last sensing he was being taken seriously. As far as the Kent Police were concerned, Vincent knew they had a main suspect in the form of Colin Ash-Smith and that they had been focused on him since the attack on Charlotte Barnard in 1995. However, he felt through his research that Napper was a better suspect for the Tiltman murder. The irony of the parallels to the Nickell case were not lost on Vincent as, at this meeting, it was again explained to him how Kent Police had a chief suspect and were not looking for anyone else. Although at this stage Ash-Smith had still not been charged with Claire Tiltman's murder, many police officers and members of the public had found him guilty in their own minds.

Things quietened down in 2008 with the conviction of Robert Napper for the murder of Rachel Nickell. Naturally it was massive news but, in the round of congratulations, Vincent was left on the sidelines without any acknowledgement of his contribution. His private investigation into the Tiltman case had reached an impasse. Despite trying to obtain further information via the Freedom of Information Act he found his requests thwarted at every stage. Then he tried a new tack. He contacted universities with law and psychology faculties to try and interest them in taking on the Tiltman case as an 'innocence project'. Some universities had adopted this approach as part of their courses to encourage students to re-examine cases and all the available evidence in an effort to identify miscarriages of justice. None of them showed any interest in the Tiltman case.

As described in *Chapter 16*, in 2012 Vincent was contacted by a film company who specialised in crime documentaries asking him if he would assist them in making a programme on the Tiltman case. This was broadcast on Channel 5 in 2013 in the series *Killers Behind Bars*. It was fronted by Professor David Wilson who regularly asked his students to examine the known evidence from the trials of convicted killers to link them to other possible murders. Not unlike the premise of Operation Enigma undertaken by the Metropolitan Police some years before.

One of the episodes featured none other than Robert Napper. The programme went on to describe the links between Napper's known offences and the murders of Jean Bradley and Claire Tiltman. Although presented in a dramatic way the programme did raise some valid points. It included crime scene visits and an analysis of Napper's whereabouts at the time of each murder. These revelations caused hardly a ripple in the public consciousness and may be viewed now as an interesting curio. The premise of Napper having killed Claire Tiltman received a serious blow when, in 2014, Colin Ash-Smith was charged with her murder and convicted in December of the same year. Just prior to that trial, demonstrating a belief in his suspicions far beyond the ordinary, Vincent Wright wrote again to the Kent Police asking them to consider Napper as a viable suspect. He received a polite 'Thank you for your continued interest' letter, but nothing more.

The parallels with the Nickell case were quite startling by now. When the Nickell investigation was first approached in 1994 by the Bisset investigation team expressing their suspicions about the possibility of Napper being responsible for the murder of Rachel Nickell, their response went beyond dismissive and could even be described as hostile. Each of the investigating teams of Nickell and Tiltman had their man and were not to be distracted in their quest to prove their own suspects guilty. In Nickell's case, Colin Stagg, in Tiltman's Colin Ash-Smith.

In October 2014, one month prior to the trial of Ash-Smith for the murder of Claire Tiltman, Vincent contacted the defence team via their solicitors, Carringtons based in Nottingham. By this stage and after so much research he was convinced that Ash-Smith had not killed Claire and he wanted to share his concerns with them before the forthcoming trial, and to gauge what 'defence' they would be using. A meeting was arranged with Ash-Smith's representative, Nadir Prabatani, and Vincent made the journey to Nottingham to meet him. The meeting, at Prabatani's request, was conducted in a public house which Vincent felt gave it a rather 'clandestine' air. Vincent voiced his concerns over the case against Ash-Smith and laid out his reasons why he thought Napper was a much more likely suspect. Prabatani listened with interest then suggested a meeting be arranged between Vincent and defence counsel, David Nathan QC. That meeting never materialised. I do not know whether they were interested in Vincent's theories, if of course they or anyone else in a position to influence Ash-Smith's defence, got to hear of them. But it seems that professional practitioners generally do not take well to outsiders 'meddling' in their affairs and as I mentioned in an earlier chapter Vincent had on at least one occasion been made to feel like a 'nutter'. There is also of course the issue of client confidentiality which tends to keep information within a protective bubble.

As described in *Chapter 17*, the trial went ahead, Ash-Smith was found guilty and in December 2014 was sentenced by Mr Justice Sweeney to life imprisonment.[13] A result which amazed Vincent, not only by the finality of matters but because of what seemed to both him and myself to be a lack of real fight to avoid a 'guilty' outcome. I should allow for the fact here that defence tactics may have many considerations, legal and otherwise, so I had better just say that Vincent disagreed with the

13. The text of Mr Justice Sweeney's sentencing remarks can be found at https://www.judiciary.uk/wp-content/uploads/2014/12/ash-smith-sentencing-remarks.pdf Strong in condemnation of Colin Ash-Smith it must be borne in mind that they followed from conviction by the jury and so are based on the prosecution version of events which this book challenges.

defence approach. However, if the case I make in this book is correct, I believe he had ample grounds for doing so.

After the trial, Vincent decided that the only way to take his misgivings any further forward was to contact the family of Colin Ash-Smith. So it was that in early 2015 he found himself on the doorstep of Colin's parents, Diane and Aubrey. Vincent was in a quandary about doing this, like many people he couldn't feel too much sympathy for a man who, it was known, had viciously attacked two innocent women. But as Vincent has said on many occasions, 'It wasn't about Colin Ash-Smith. It was about justice for Claire Tiltman ... and still is.' He believed Colin Ash-Smith had suffered a miscarriage of justice and he wanted to offer Diane and Aubrey his support. Unsure of how he would be received, he knocked boldly on the door of the Ash-Smiths where he was met by the growls and barks of a small dog, which frantically tried to reach him through the closed door.

It was apparent the Ash-Smiths were not at home. Having come prepared for this eventuality Vincent posted a letter explaining his visit through their letter box. Whereupon, without a moment's hesitation, the letter was gratefully and energetically seized by the small dog. A neighbour was working on his van in the next driveway and slid out from underneath the vehicle to pronounce to Vincent, 'They are out. And Aubrey doesn't like journalists.' He thanked him and said, 'I am neither a journalist nor a police officer. If you could just ask Aubrey to read the letter and to contact me.'

Without any great expectations, Vincent awaited a response. Then, after a few days he received a text from Diane Ash-Smith. The dog had left sufficient remains of the letter for her to decipher the contents. She was interested in what Vincent had to say and she wanted to know more. After he had explained in detail his interest to the Ash-Smiths he found they were pleased to have an ally in their cause. He explained how he had no financial interest. It was purely out of his sense of justice that he had pursued the case for so long. This was the first time since Colin's arrest in 1995 that Diane and Aubrey Ash-Smith felt that someone actually believed them, that Colin was indeed with them on the night and at the time Claire was murdered.

The positive contact with the Ash-Smiths raised the game and provided fresh impetus to Vincent. He wrote to the court asking for the trial transcripts and to Colin Ash-Smith in prison to gain his permission to obtain the defence papers from Carringtons solicitors. The transcripts would not be released without payment of several thousands of pounds, a premise which was out of the question. However, the defence papers were made available by Carringtons and these Vincent picked up from their offices in Nottingham. The files contained a wealth of hitherto unknown (to him) information including thousands of files, statements, scientific and pathology reports as well as photographs. At the same time, he had written to a charity called Inside Justice which specialised in miscarriages of justice. He was introduced to its founder Louise Shorter. Louise, because of her current workload could not take up the case but did arrange an introduction for Vincent to meet Dr Stephen Heaton at the Law Department of the University of East Anglia. Dr Heaton agreed to take on the case as an 'innocence project' for his undergraduates to cut their teeth on.

After having approached ten other universities without success Vincent was pleased to have the University of East Anglia take on the project. Dr Heaton introduced a caveat that Vincent must step aside and take no part in it. He accepted this, being only too pleased that some progress was being made. A meeting was arranged in Norwich in the Spring of 2016. This took place in a country car park, some miles from the university campus. Another reflection perhaps of the attitude of some of those connected to this case sensing they were involved in and carrying out some type of undercover work. Nevertheless, Vincent again handed over to someone who was a complete stranger and in trust all of his research on the Tiltman case. He believed that the university would soon identify the many anomalies in the case. After all they were now all singing from the same hymn sheet.

Vincent heard nothing for over 12 months until, in the middle of 2017, he received a letter from Dr Heaton with an attached letter of rejection from the Criminal Case Review Commission. The CCRC's letter largely reiterated the allegations and the findings of the Crown Court and Court of Appeal. An opportunity had been missed and progress towards correcting a perceived injustice had been delayed for another year.

At about this time the BBC broadcast its programme *The Prosecutors* described in *Chapter 17* about the CPS at work, a part of which covered the Tiltman case and showed Ash-Smith in a very poor light.

On 19 March 2018 the CCRC ruling was sent to Colin Ash-Smith at his prison, HMP Frankland, near Durham. It wasn't good news as far as he was concerned. The CCRC did not support a review of his conviction, nor any referral back to the Court of Appeal. The reasons given and addressed to Ash-Smith were (paraphrased)

- At the trial it was alleged you repeatedly stabbed Claire Tiltman in an alleyway.
- The prosecution relied upon circumstantial and bad character evidence.
- On 18 May 2015 your application was referred by a single judge who said evidence had been properly submitted and relied upon.
- Even in the absence of 'bad character evidence' the evidence against you was very powerful.[14]

Not deterred Vincent began with a new tack by approaching forensic pathologists for their advice. This also seemed to be a dead end as initially no replies were forthcoming. In the medical profession it is hard

14. The full text of the CCRC's findings (stamped 'Confidential') is not in the public domain. I have, however, had sight of this document courtesy of the defence papers kindly provided to Vincent Wright by Carrington's defence solicitors. The document is confined to key points and a rejection of all those raised in challenging the conviction. A 'regurgitation' of the status quo based on the prosecution version of events, the verdict of the Crown Court, Mr Justice Sweeney's sentencing remarks and the refusal of the Court of Appeal to allow Ash-Smith to pursue the matter further in the courts. Whereas the text of this book concerns known and provable facts and weaknesses or mistakes in the evidence or arguments leading to conviction, the CCRC is dismissive as per the following extract: 'The CCRC has had access to Kent Constabulary HOLMES ... account which contains the information gathered during the investigation. This has been interrogated by the CCRC in relation to enquiries made in relation to [other] individuals and any other potential suspects and persons of interest. The investigations undertaken were thorough and appropriate and the CCRC has not identified any additional lines of enquiry that should reasonably have been undertaken.' I have listed why I believe such enquiries were not 'thorough' and 'lines of enquiry' not yet pursued in *Chapter 21*.

enough to persuade one doctor to give an opinion of another's work. In the field of forensic pathology this is intensified. However, there was one responder, Professor James Grieve, a senior forensic pathologist from Scotland. Grieve raised tacit support for questioning the apparent strangeness of the three-year gap between Dr Heath's original post mortem report and his new report, made in November 1995 (*Chapter 13*). A report in which Heath had asserted:

> 'It is my opinion that Claire Tiltman was attacked by an assailant with a knife in his left hand. This indicates that the assailant was left-handed.'

This second report was written only after Kent Police asked Dr Heath, soon after their arrest of Ash-Smith, to physically examine victims Beverley Godfrey and Charlotte Bernard. The two women Ash-Smith confessed to attacking. Colin Ash-Smith their left-handed suspect!

In 2019, my first book, *Napper: Through a Glass Darkly* was published. As I mentioned in the *Introduction* to this work, Vincent Wright immediately saw how it offered him new information to take the Tiltman case forward. Through my publishers he made contact and we met to discuss aspects of that book which threw light on the Tiltman enquiry. In particular, the knives bought by Napper on two occasions. One shortly before Rachel Nickell was killed and another in the weeks prior to the murder of Claire. That particular knife was delivered to Napper's address in Plumstead in December 1992 (just three weeks before the Tiltman murder). The knife was identical to the one he purchased just days before Rachel Nickell's death, an SOG military sheath knife at a cost of £60 (even in 1992!). None of these knives have ever been recovered, including the one used to kill Samantha Bisset. It has long been suspected they are still hidden in a stash somewhere. Napper did collect trophies and a biscuit tin was recovered having been buried in woodland which contained one of his firearms. It is not beyond the bounds of possibility there are still hidden boxes of incriminating evidence waiting to be found.

Then there were the similarities of the wounds inflicted on Claire and Rachel. Both with extreme force, leaving hilt marks on the skin, both using a hunting military-type knife. Just the type Napper was wont to purchase. In July 2020, Vincent made a final attempt to interest the Kent Police and met two detectives at Northfleet Police Station, one of whom had worked on the Tiltman case for many years. Although again politely received, without preamble he was informed that Kent Police were satisfied with their investigation of Ash-Smith and that the conviction was sound. The detectives were not interested in the anomalies of Dr Heath's report into left-handedness or of considering another possible suspect, i.e. Napper.

When Vincent contacted me, I must admit that at first I was rather taken aback. We on the Bisset investigation had considered other possible victims for Napper and the name Tiltman had been mentioned during the enquiry. Naturally so, as it was a very unusual attack on a defenceless female in an area not far from where Napper was operating. It must be remembered that Claire was murdered eleven months before the Bissets were killed in Plumstead and subsequent to the Bisset investigation there was antipathy towards believing he could have travelled across London to murder Rachel Nickell. A theory which wasn't to be demonstrated as indisputably wrong for another 15 years.

However, the story and enthusiasm of Vincent Wright at least ignited the interest within me to look further into the possibilities of the case. I remained sceptical with my maxim of, 'It is one thing to cast doubt on a person's guilt, quite another to confidently transfer the guilt to another person without falling into the same trap that led to the allegations being made against the original suspect.'

CHAPTER 20

The Polygraph: Is it All Lies?

I decided, upon hearing the case made by Vincent Wright, to carry out my own research. Naturally, without any formal position and having long retired as a detective, I had limited access to material to conduct a formal review. I have conducted many of these in the past and they follow the form of examining the detail, which in turn will identify any shortfalls or avenues for further investigation. Once these have been identified, the reviewer will then present a case with recommendations to be submitted, in the case of the Metropolitan Police, to a crime panel who study the review, assess its worth and authorise either a limited or full investigation. At least, through Vincent, I had access to hundreds of statements and reports which he had managed to obtain.

I didn't have access to everything, but I could see most of the relevant paperwork. I came to the conclusion I should meet Diane Ash-Smith. I reasoned from the early stages of my own research that this case rested not on whether Colin Ash-Smith was referring to the zebra crossing in London Road (as laid out by prosecuting counsel). Rather, was he with his mother and father in their house in Milton Street, Swanscombe at the relevant time on the evening of the murder. If it could be established beyond doubt that he was in his house at the time of Claire's murder (a time which could be pinpointed to within two or three minutes: see *Chapter 18*) then he could not have committed the murder.

Through Vincent, I arranged to meet Diane Ash-Smith, who I was surprised to discover he had never met in person. All of their contact had been by telephone, text and email. He explained this as wishing to maintain a distance from the case which would help him preserve his judgement and perspective. My meeting with her was arranged for the

23 February 2021 in the foyer of the Hilton Hotel, Dartford. These cold meetings can be difficult and unpredictable but after years of experience meeting witnesses in such circumstances in the police it held no fears for me. What I had to remember was, how did it seem through her eyes? I needn't have worried, and recognising her from her photograph we met in the foyer and the ice was soon broken as over a cup of coffee we discussed the case.

I found Diane Ash-Smith to be quick, alert and open. When asked directly if she was with Colin on the evening of the murder she was unhesitating in her affirmative response. I found her believable in all the answers she provided. She was open and honest about the terrible crimes committed by her son but was emphatic that it couldn't have been Colin who killed Claire. I am not going to claim that just because someone tells me a story in a believable manner it follows that it is true. I have interviewed far too many convincing liars to be able to believe that of myself. The purpose of such meetings is to lay the groundwork in order to be able to check on whether or not any evidence backs up the claims made. Nevertheless, my interview with Diane Ash-Smith did spur me on to investigate further and to ponder just why she hadn't been called to give her alibi evidence in court.

After the interview we decided to ask Diane Ash-Smith if she was prepared to take a polygraph test. This is something I had never used during all my police service and which certainly in the past was frowned upon by many of my colleagues as something unreliable. It is certainly true that the polygraph cannot be used as evidence in any criminal court in the UK. However, a little research showed that it is used within the modern legal system, including currently for the assessment of sex-offenders on licence.

It is relevant to examine the history and use of the polygraph within the Criminal Justice System. Although earlier attempts had been made, the person credited with inventing it was an American police officer, John Larson, in 1921. Officer Larson had a penchant for science and developed an application which was capable of simultaneously measuring changes in blood pressure, heart rate and respiratory rate. Larson's objective was to aid detection in cases of deception. A brilliant concept but one almost immediately mired in controversy. Larson's original concept was soon taken up by the press and re-named 'the lie detector'. An epithet which unfortunately stuck.

The major problem with the equipment and the results it gave was that it could never be 100% accurate and there was always room for error. To compare this to the development in the fight against crime of fingerprints and DNA, the polygraph was always going to be the poor cousin. As the banks of fingerprints and DNA profiles lent ever more proof to their infallibility, the same could not be said of the polygraph. The cautious attitude to polygraph testing was exacerbated by the actions of those who were only interested in making quick money at the expense of scientific integrity.

In 1983, the polygraph came back into the headlines when US President Ronald Reagan issued National Security Directive 84. This authorised polygraph tests to be given to government employees to detect whether they had leaked information. There followed three months of furious protest by Government workers which culminated in the withdrawal of the directive. The US Government tried to reintroduce the polygraph for the same security reasons in February 2015. It was initially trumpeted as a triumph of science which would 'alter the investigation of crime for ever'.

The polygraph has consistently failed to live up to expectations. This is hardly surprising, as the test was expected by some to be infallible. This was never and never has been the case and in the current scientific climate its use was always to be viewed with caution. The modern polygraph may be summed up as a device to test and discriminate lies from truth, giving results at rates well beyond chance. An ambition with a bar set well below perfection.

The polygraph's worth has veered wildly over the years as a war between academics and those focused on its lucrative potential holds back proper research and scientific rigour. It has suffered as a result of its own initial fame and the perception of a 'lie detector' having been invented. The modern version of the test gives an accuracy rating of between 80% and 90% and records a number of body responses: blood pressure, breathing patterns and palm sweating. It is based on the principal of 'fight or flight', a deep-rooted animal response inherent in all of us. Polygraphs do not measure deception or lying directly but by behavioural and physiological changes which may then be interpreted by a trained operator.

Having laid out the negative side of the history, use and abuse of the polygraph, when it is used in the proper circumstances it is a valid and useful tool. It is worthless as something to use when interviewing suspects along the lines of, 'Did you do it? No, I didn't.' However, adapt its use to determining the subtle use of deception and we are in a different sphere. Having researched the use of polygraphs, a decision was needed to establish what the value of its use in the Tiltman case was. I contacted an old friend, Tom Simmons QPM, who, after retiring from the police, had developed a company which used the polygraph in determining the safety of those having charge over vulnerable children. From what he told me the feedback was encouraging.

As a tool in the investigation of crime, it is still unacceptable to use polygraph evidence under UK law. However, Tom had been employed using the polygraph test to interview potential workers with vulnerable young people. This had been brought to a head after several national scandals involving large organizations such as the scouting movement and football academies employing unsuitable people who had lied during their job interviews. The use of polygraphs and the possibility of cheating the system are neatly summed up by a leading authority on their current use, Professor Don Grubin, who said, 'You can cheat the system, but this requires knowledge and training.'

Although polygraph testing remains outside the sphere of evidence required in the criminal courts, its use is now enshrined in English law under the Offender Management Act 2007. This allows polygraph testing to monitor serious sex-offenders who are on parole. In 2014 this became compulsory for high-risk offenders.

Tom Simmons was no longer working in this field but put me in touch with Rod (known by all as Ned) Kelly a retired police officer from Essex who had started his own company R D Kelly Consulting Ltd, using the polygraph test. It was a field in which he had carried out a lot of work for the Essex Police whilst he was still serving. He was now employed by companies around the world who wanted his expertise. After contacting Kelly, he agreed to take on the case. Diane Ash-Smith was very keen to undergo it as was her son Colin. The first stumbling block was the fee. At £750 for each test, just with Diane plus the hire of a suitable venue it wasn't going to be cheap. She immediately said she would pay for it but I reasoned if we also did a test on Colin the cost would be considerably more because of the simple logistics. At the time, his test would have to be arranged within HMP Frankland near Durham and Ned would need to travel there to do it. We also had to have the agreement of the prison authorities. In fact this has never been forthcoming despite Colin's desire to undertake a polygraph test.

I had been in contact with the Ferrari Press News Agency. They were very interested in the story of the Tiltman murder. Consequently, I arranged a meeting with them to explain the circumstances, after which they agreed to pay for the polygraph test on Diane. I reasoned that we would await the result of that test before pursuing the test with Colin Ash-Smith as, if she failed it, there wouldn't be any point in continuing the exercise. I gave Ned the go ahead and arranged a room for the test to be held in St Mary's Community Hall, Eltham. On the 27 January 2022 there, I met with Diane Ash-Smith and introduced her to Ned Kelly. Also present was Vincent Wright who was about to meet Diane for the first time. After the introductions, Vincent and I departed to a local café while Ned continued with the test on Diane.

We had prepared beforehand a synopsis of the case for Ned and a list of crucial questions. How he conducted the test was absolutely a matter for him under the guidelines of Behavioural Measures UK, the controlling body for polygraph tests in the UK. This entailed a pre-test interview. It began in Diane's case with the regular series of questions about her personal circumstances, followed by questions about her life in Greenhithe at the relevant time in 1993. She replied that in 1993 she was living in Swanscombe with her husband Aubrey and son Colin where she was a local town and borough councillor. When asked about her knowledge of Claire Tiltman she explained that she, her husband and her son Colin knew Claire and the Tiltman family through them all belonging to the British Legion Club. Aubrey Ash-Smith probably knew them best. Colin played a lot of pool at the club and had played the game with Claire who was an accomplished player. The two families did not mix socially but were well acquainted.

The test then turned to the more crucial area of what she was doing on the night of Claire's murder. She told Ned she had not gone to work that day as she had been feeling poorly. She had stayed at home and prepared some letters in her capacity as a councillor to deliver locally. At this time, she could not drive so waited for her son Colin to arrive home from work so he could give her a lift to deliver the letters. This was normal practice for them, and Colin would have expected to be asked to do it. He arrived home at some time between 5 pm and 6 pm and she asked him to drive her to deliver a letter to Edward (Ted) Wells in Eynsford Road, Greenhithe, a short drive from their house. Colin drove her to Eynsford Road in his white Ford Capri where Diane delivered the letter through Mr Wells' letter box and Colin waited a few moments for her to return to the waiting car. Both Ted Wells and Colin thought that must have happened, but it must be borne in mind that Diane was a frequent visitor to the house of Ted Wells who, on his own admission, was a person in regular contact with the council over various issues. What actually happened on that day may have become confused but what can be said with certainty is that the visit was of short duration and Colin stayed outside Ted Wells' house in his car waiting for his mother. They then drove off together in his Ford Capri. The whole trip took no more than ten minutes. As already noted, Colin had waited in the car outside Mr Well's house and then they both drove straight home, where they remained for the rest of the evening.

Diane told how she heard of the death of Claire the following day. She summarised her son's convictions for sexual assault and attempted murder in 1988 (Godfrey attack) and grievous bodily harm in 1995 (Barnard attack) and how it had led to Aubrey and herself being charged with attempting to pervert the course of justice relating to the subsequent charging and conviction of Colin for the murder of Claire. Diane had always kept a bowl full of 'bits and bobs' and in this bowl was a penknife. After Colin had been arrested and questioned over Claire's murder, Aubrey became paranoid and destroyed the penknife. She had told him to, 'Get rid of it.' But this 'throwaway' comment was born out of worry and paranoia after they felt the police were convinced Colin had killed Claire. During the interview Diane hadn't disclosed anything which she had not previously stated, and she remained absolutely adamant that she and Colin were together during the time of Claire's murder.

The test, having been concluded, was given the following assessment:

> 'Conclusion
>
> Diane Ash-Smith did not show significant responses to the questions asked in this polygraph test and is assessed as having answered the questions truthfully.
>
> Diane has been consistent in maintaining her position that she was in the company of her son Colin Ash-Smith at the time of Claire Tiltman's murder. I found no contradictions during her interview and the polygraph examination supports her claim.
>
> The polygraph examination has been subject to quality control and the outcome of the test has been supported.'

We had successfully managed the first hurdle. According to a subjective polygraph test, Diane Ash-Smith was telling the truth about Colin Ash-Smith being in her company for the entire evening of 18 January 1993. The assessment was given an 80% factor of the likelihood of being an accurate summary of events. This figure of 80% is always rounded down to the lowest denominator. As explained, the test is not infallible, but is without doubt an indictor of whether the person performing the test is attempting to be deceitful. The beauty of this exercise is the that if two people are telling the same story of the same event, statistics show that if both pass the test as being truthful and both achieve scores of 80%, then their combined likelihood of telling the truth increases to 96%. The next step in this regard must be to persuade HM Prison Service to allow a polygraph test on Colin Ash-Smith. An agreement with which he concurs and has demanded.

It is of great concern that Diane Ash-Smith was prevented from giving her evidence of alibi at the trial and not allowed to take her chances in the witness box. The reason given, that she would not be able to stand up to the prosecution's questioning is not valid and far from being dissuaded from giving evidence during the trial she should have been encouraged and lawfully prepared for the event. Her evidence of alibi was crucial to this case and (as required by the laws of criminal procedure) notice should have been given to the court at the earliest possible stage that an alibi might be raised so as to allow the police to look into and assess this specifically. Alibi is an 'all or nothing' defence but Colin must have known this from the moment he told the police he was at home with his parents. It is also an obvious answer for someone being asked about their whereabouts at any given moment. Seemingly, not raising his mother's alibi evidence was a deliberate tactic on the part of the defence but, if so, I cannot see whatever was the advantage of it.

CHAPTER 21

Summary and Weighing the Balance

Mr Pip: 'I always supposed it was Miss Haversham.'
Mr Jaggers: 'There's not a particle of evidence. Take nothing on its looks. Take everything on evidence.'— On Pip meeting his lawyer, Jaggers, *Great Expectations*, Charles Dickens (1812–1870)

From an early standpoint of scepticism about the innocence of Colin Ash-Smith concerning the murder of Claire Tiltman, I gradually moved—after considering the many factors which cast shadows of doubt upon his guilt—to a position of believing there may have been a miscarriage of justice. The case for his conviction is on the face of it plausible. Any murder squad detective who has such a suspect thrown into their lap would be keen to follow the facts and prove his guilt. After the murder, nearly three years went by before his name came into the 'suspect' category, but when it did, it did so for good reason. He had committed two not dissimilar—albeit sexual offences—and they were both stranger attacks against women within the small locale of Greenhithe.

Taking the principle of Dickens' character Mr Jaggers, never mind how things appear but please consider exactly what was (and is) the evidence against Colin Ash-Smith?

Forensics

The murder scene produced absolutely no forensic links to him. Naturally, investigators were keen to redress this, and, on his arrest, large quantities of his clothing were seized in the hope of finding some trace of a forensic connection between Claire and him. As time had moved on, subtle advances were being made in the use of DNA evidence in criminal cases and the power of that evidence was becoming ever more refined, as demonstrated to spectacular effect in the Rachel Nickell case. The Tiltman murder team had high hopes that a forensic link would be made between Ash-Smith and Claire. Yet, despite rigorous comparisons between the clothing of both no such link was ever made.

Lapse of time

The time which passed between the date of the murder and suspicion falling on Ash-Smith must be taken into account, balanced by the fact that, as far as can be established, he had made no effort to dispose of any of his clothing. Also, bear in mind that he was still in possession on his arrest of a school tie which (as he freely admitted) he had used in the abduction and attempted rape of Beverley Godfrey back in 1988. Hardly the actions of a forensically aware person. As already indicated, despite high hopes and some false indications of a possible forensic link, none was ever made.

Left-handedness

Without any forensic evidence, the testimony of pathologist Dr Michael Heath of the left-handedness of the assailant became ever more crucial to the case. His re-evaluation of his original post-mortem almost three years after the event and subsequent to the arrest of Ash-Smith introduced his opinion that the assailant was left-handed. Whatever his professional credentials, this neatly coincided with the fact that Ash-Smith was indeed left-handed. This fact alone narrowed the potential suspects down to between 8% and 10% of the population.

Dr Heath, in his summary of his re-evaluation of the murder, gave no reasons publicly for his conclusion that the assailant was left-handed so far as I can establish and his evidence wasn't challenged in the murder trial.[15] As an expert witness, his opinion is valid and may be accepted in court as evidence. It is usual in such cases to have such evidence corroborated by a second opinion. A second pathologist was asked to ratify Dr Heath's opinion. However, the second doctor merely corroborated the findings of the original post-mortem. The investigating team did not push this further and accepted at face value that the assailant who attacked Claire must have been left-handed.

A further opinion was sought from two other doctors, Professor Vanezis, who backed Heath's conclusions, and Dr David Rouse who was neutral in his assessment. Although the temptation must have been overwhelming to proceed on this basis, I believe it was a grave mistake and an oversight (or tactical mistake) by the defence team. If it had been my case, I would have expected a vigorous challenge in the subsequent trial and taken steps to solidly corroborate the evidence of Dr Heath. Amazingly a challenge was never forthcoming.

Experts generally

It is a temptation in criminal investigations to apportion too much credence to the findings and opinions of experts. It has often been my experience that the awaited result from a scientist to harden the evidence in a case can be a disappointment, or even worse, a bland statement saying, in effect, 'nothing further can be done'. Investigators should be aware of and always pursue such 'gaps', taking alternative paths if necessary. Only when every avenue has been explored to its limits can they have the right to feel they have completed their task, however much it may raise the prospect of disappointment.

Eye-witnesses

Without compelling or uncontentious forensic evidence the prosecutor must turn to witness evidence. It is beyond dispute that no-one saw

15. As noted in *Chapter 12*, the details and direction of the stab wounds and where the perpetrator may have been standing in relation to the victim were mentioned in his original report but there was nothing about 'handedness'.

the crime being committed, therefore the next best thing should be to identify suspects in the vicinity, either immediately before or immediately after the event. There were several sightings of a person behaving suspiciously in London Road just prior to the murder. There are also sightings of a suspect immediately after the event, in Riverview Road and near Greenhithe Railway Station. The list of witnesses is a long one. Danny French, Lee Hooper, Kathleen Still, Julie Driscoll, Christine Doyle, Donna Newstead, Lee Delguidice, Diane and Glenn Eversfield, Paul Harris, Gitte Hansen, Jaqueline Gower and Raymond Hurt, plus eleven more. All these individuals gave descriptions of a suspect and provided statements to the police. The more relevant ones have been dealt with in detail earlier in this book and their timed sightings in *Chapter 18*:

- Sightings of a man who couldn't universally be described as definitely the same man. But what we can determine is that not one of these witnesses picked out local man Colin Ash-Smith in all the subsequent identity parades. The general opinion was, however, that he was wearing a light or tan-coloured top. Anorak-style but not padded and not elasticated at the waist. This suspect was also reported as having a strange gait or limp (just like Napper when seen near the Nickell murder). Wearing white training boots (Napper wore white Adidas low cut basketball boots at the Bisset murders) and jeans (Ash-Smith did not wear and did not possess a pair of jeans). No similar articles were found in any of the searches of premises where Ash-Smith had access.

- Of the witnesses who came forward not one of them was able to identify Ash-Smith as being in the vicinity at or about the time of the murder. There is no indication at all that he was there at the relevant time. The only information of the whereabouts of Ash-Smith at that time puts him elsewhere, i.e. at his home address. Information that the defence declined to use in the trial (*Chapter 17*). In contrast, it should also be borne in mind that when Ash-Smith attacked Charlotte Barnard in 1995 (coincidentally at the same time in the evening and within a few hundred yards of the scene of the Tiltman murder) there was no shortage of witnesses giving a good description of both him and his car so that he was arrested within six hours. Descriptions which were later confirmed at identity parades.

Propensity

Other prosecution evidence in this case was reliant on prosecutors showing what can be summarised as a propensity to misconduct (or lying) on the part of Ash-Smith that aided understanding as to why, as it was alleged, he committed murder. As mentioned in *Chapter 17*, to this end and pursuant to the Criminal Justice Act 2003 (which replaced the former common law doctrine of 'similar fact evidence') prosecutors obtained the trial judge's consent to introduce evidence of 'bad character', viz his convictions for and details of his attacks on Beverley Godfrey (December 1988) and Charlotte Barnard (October 1995) before his 2014 trial for the January 1993 murder of Claire Tiltman.

The idea behind the new law was to repair a loophole that caused public alarm about (perceived) miscarriages of justice in terms of acquittal. Until 2003, there was no statutory mechanism allowing a jury to learn how often a suspect may have committed a similar offence something that under the historic common law rule (often lauded as a fundamental legal principle) could only occur in extremely limited circumstances.

It is worth adding here that the 2003 Act, subject to the judge's discretion, allows evidence of lies by an accused person to be given in evidence in support of bad character (i.e. not just evidence of earlier offences). However, it seems to go without saying that simply denying the charge on which a person is arrested or being tried (in Ash-Smith's case Claire's murder) cannot in itself be deemed to be lying for this purpose. Else everyone pleading not guilty would be affected and this would undermine their right to a fair trial. It is tantamount to saying 'plead not guilty and because we say it is a lie we will use that against you.'[16] I have already emphasised that Ash-Smith was wholly forthcoming about his existing offences (just two remember, the attacks on Charlotte and Beverley). He may, as already described in this book, have occasionally been mistaken or hazy in distant, several years' old recollections. But nowhere can I find reliable or other evidence of him lying. Only, at best, questionable claims that he had lied by those seeking to convict him of murder.

The other point I should make here is that there is every difference in the world between saying that evidence is *admissible* under the bad character provisions of the 2003 Act and how much *weight* should be attached to such evidence once allowed in. This is part of the same issue as whether, e.g. previous convictions and weak circumstantial evidence can somehow support each other as part of some greater whole (see also the next heading). It is my contention that throughout this case these two distinct aspects became confused and greater reliance than was justified was placed on so-called 'bad character' so that, e.g. dissimilarities were not sufficiently recognised.

Indeed, the 2003 Act itself has many safeguards to avoid such evidence being used in unfair circumstances but is debatable whether they protected Ash-Smith in his 2014 trial for murder. The main limitation is that prosecutors cannot rely on bad character exclusively, but only to reinforce other evidence. This 'other evidence' must naturally be sound. As a regular and experienced investigator and reviewer of serious crime, I know all too well that evidence of bad character is worthless if backed only by weak circumstantial evidence. I believe there was no strong, or sufficiently reliable, other evidence (see also the next heading).

The evidence of bad character should be revisited. It would appear from the trial papers that despite initial optimism about further evidence coming to light to support a prosecution (viz the CPS belief that witnesses would materialise who saw Ash-Smith in London Road and that other

16. Nonetheless, Mr Justice Sweeney in his sentencing remarks appears to have equated Colin Ash-Smith's denial that he attacked Claire with lying, something also implicitly accepted by the Court of Appeal and CCRC. Under the 2003 Act, lying within the proceedings cannot amount to bad character evidence (see section 98) although it is admissible under the general law of evidence. Even so, where from start to finish of the proceedings against Ash-Smith is the evidence of him lying unless already deemed to be guilty?

witnesses would come forward saying they saw his distinctive white Ford Capri in the area at the relevant time), the prosecution ended up relying far too heavily on his existing convictions—propensity evidence—and in a way likely to influence a jury unfairly. This is not I believe how the Criminal Justice Act 2003 was ever meant to be interpreted and this may in itself be sufficient grounds to apply for a re-trial. Especially if considered well away from the frenetic activity that drove the perceived need to make sure Colin Ash-Smith was not released on parole in 2014.

Weak evidence

The CPS decided, just as Ash-Smith was approaching his first chance of parole, that they would charge him with the murder of Claire Tiltman. In *Chapter 17* it can be seen from my description of the BBC TV documentary *The Prosecutors* that the CPS hoped a witness would materialise who would put Ash-Smith and his distinctive Ford Capri at or near the murder scene at the relevant time. This never happened. The police meanwhile had been given some encouragement that further forensic evidence utilising new DNA techniques would also link Ash-Smith to Claire Tiltman. This also failed to materialise. In what appears to have been 'desperation', the prosecution turned to cell confession evidence. This is another area littered with booby traps and best avoided if at all possible.

There is no knowing what the motivation of one prisoner may be to give evidence against another including that the latter has privately confessed in his cell. The witness Stefan Dubois (who had an adjacent cell to Ash-Smith) was relied upon to give evidence that Ash-Smith had confessed to him he had murdered Claire. Looked at in more detail, the 'confession' not only doesn't make sense, it's not a confession at all. Even if, unlike with many such cell confessions, Dubois did not have any apparent motive to point the finger at Ash-Smith. By the time police caught up with Dubois he had completed his sentence and was making a good attempt at reintegrating himself into society. He had a job and had steered clear of criminal activity. Furthermore, Dubois and Ash-Smith had become friends and Dubois even visited Ash-Smith in prison after Dubois had completed his sentence and his release.

The person 'seen' on the zebra crossing

Another line of 'evidence' used against Ash-Smith was the inference drawn by investigators from a witness statement provided by Ash-Smith one week after Claire's murder. In it he describes an unknown person near the zebra crossing. This was interpreted by investigators to mean that he had deliberately said this in order to give himself an alibi. By 'describing someone in place of himself'. If so, it is a poor show as he could not tell if the person was male or female and the person had dark curly hair (A reference to the police photograph of Ash-Smith shows there is no comparison).

The crux of the so-called 'cell confession' by Stefan Dubois was that he said that Ash-Smith, when describing one of his sexual attacks, had mentioned it was near to a zebra crossing. The prosecution seized upon this, pointing out that neither of the two other offences attributed to Ash-Smith were near zebra crossings. But that there was a zebra crossing at the top of London Road, which Ash-Smith himself had mentioned in his first witness statement to the police. This piece of information was somehow conflated into, 'If there were no zebra crossings in the other offences, and there was a zebra crossing near to the Tiltman murder, this must mean the zebra crossing referred to was the one in London Road'. Here it was supposed by the CPS that Ash-Smith saw Claire Tiltman, got out of his Capri, then followed her down London Road and killed her in the alleyway. A bit of a jump in the direction of 'circumstantial supposition', but readily 'swallowed' by the jury.

When Dubois found out to his horror his statement was being used for this purpose he spoke over the telephone to Ash-Smith in prison to apologise. The conversation was recorded, Ash-Smith was quite conciliatory and told Dubois not to worry about it. Hardly the expected reaction to the report that Dubois was giving evidence of a cell confession. However, the prosecution pinned their hopes on the evidence of Dubois. He was called as a witness during the trial and, as has previously been described, repeated the fact that on no occasion did Ash-Smith ever admit the murder of Claire Tiltman to him or to anyone else when he was present.

Contrasting the evidence: Ash-Smith v Napper

As each raft of the prosecution case starts to look less sound and certain, it is time to examine exactly what evidence there is at all to show Colin Ash-Smith's guilt. The first and obvious fact is that he had attacked two lone, defenceless females. This is beyond doubt as he has admitted both attacks and served terms of imprisonment for them. Both of those victims were attacked in the locality of Greenhithe near to where Claire was murdered. Both were subjected to violent assaults using a knife as a weapon. Both victims were unknown to their attacker.

The very fact that the three attacks were committed within such a small area is very relevant. Trying to link them all as being committed by the same attacker would be a natural progression in any investigation. But where lies any similarity? Even the two attacks Ash-Smith admitted to were not similar to one another. In the first an air-pistol was also used to subdue the victim. If the tie used in an attempt to strangle Beverley Godfrey hadn't been spotted by a keen-eyed SOCO, the two cases, which were seven years apart, might never have been linked. In both cases the victims were stabbed, but on examination of the wounds they do not appear to have the same ferocity or indeed finality as applied to Claire.

The two attacks had an obvious sexual element, something that is not immediately apparent if at all in the attack on Claire and was never alleged. There did not appear to be any other motive in the attack on Claire other than to kill her.

Both Beverley Godfrey and Charlotte Barnard were total strangers to Ash-Smith whereas he knew Claire and her family well. Nevertheless, it is an incontrovertible fact that all three violent offences were committed within a small area. As Paul Britton the clinical psychologist said of the Wimbledon Common attack on Rachel Nickell, 'I can only say that the probability of there being two people on Wimbledon Common that morning who suffered from the same extreme and violence-oriented sexual deviation is incredibly small.' This statement was based upon the assumption that Colin Stagg was a psychopathic killer, which he was later shown quite patently not to be. There was only one psychopathic killer on Wimbledon Common on the day Rachel Nickell was murdered, but it wasn't Stagg. There was only one psychopathic killer in Greenhithe on the day of Claire Tiltman's murder. But who was it really? If Colin Ash-Smith didn't murder Claire Tiltman then who did?

The man who had the opportunity and who was certainly a candidate for the application of evidence of propensity was Robert Napper. In early 1993, Napper was at the height of his psychotic paranoia. We know that during March 1992 he committed a series of progressively more violent attacks on women on the Green Chain Walk in south east London. These offences all went undetected. Once the Metropolitan Police divined a pattern to them they set up a dedicated unit to track down the offender. This had the effect of raising the profile of the attacks and making the public aware of the danger. Despite the intensity of the pursuit of the Green Chain Rapist, Napper remained free to continue with his offending. By May 1992, the Green Chain Rapes had, for no accountable reason, ceased. Operation Eccleston, set up to catch the culprit, was closed down in August that year. This, despite the fact there were still outstanding enquiries.

One final point again relating to propensity evidence (above). The post mortem on Claire Tiltman showed her to have facial bruising and a cut lip. This small fact could easily be overlooked. In almost all of the Green Chain attacks and the murder of Samantha Bisset, the victims were subjected to being punched in the face. What is clear is that Napper had stepped up a psychotic gear which resulted in the murder of Rachel Nickell on Wimbledon Common on the opposite side of London in July of 1992. This is another indisputable fact.

It must have seemed to Napper that he was unstoppable, and worse, undetectable. Despite a few scares: the request for a blood sample in September of 1992; his arrest at the end of October 1992 in Plumstead for ordering police headed notepaper from a printer in Plumstead High Street; and, during the subsequent search, the finding of a firearm at his home address, it must have seemed to Napper he could carry on planning and committing crimes with impunity.

In November 1993, he committed what was his most heinous crime, which, in the annals of Napper's offences, had to be extreme. This atrocity was the murder of Samantha Bisset and her four-year-old daughter Jazmine in their flat in Plumstead. A scene of such absolute horror mere words will never be able to describe it. The dates of Napper's offences in relation to the Tiltman murder are also significant.

During the early part of 1992 Napper committed progressively more violent rapes on females in isolated locations, some in broad daylight, some in the evening, some where the victims were accompanied by small children, others alone. In July 1992, he murdered Rachel Nickell in broad daylight in the presence of her small son on Wimbledon Common. In January 1993 Claire Tiltman was murdered in an alleyway on a dark evening. In November 1993 he murdered Samantha and Jazmine Bisset in their flat after breaking into it in the small hours.

This brief resume shows just how difficult it is to link crimes through evidence of propensity. In the cases of the rapes on the Green Chain Walk the offender left DNA which was identified as belonging to one unknown person. But what are the similarities between the Wimbledon Common and Plumstead offences? Not obvious, but subtle, and definitely there.

So by January 1993 Napper as already described was at the height of his offending. During the Bisset investigation it became apparent he was planning to commit other offences, most notably involving the young woman in Rutherglen Road and the young woman who had her gym pass stolen from the Welcome Inn pub, finding herself unknowingly, marked out in Napper's *A to Z.* There is no doubt in my mind that he was committing other offences. He is suspected of many more attacks on women during the build up of the Green Chain Walk series of rapes but was only charged with the ones where his DNA was found.

As an interviewee Napper is almost impossible to pin down. He would disrupt the proceedings by claiming he was about to have a breakdown, or he would talk about everything bar the offences. He did not admit to the Green Chain Rapes in interview or to the murders of Samantha and Jazmine. He kept that back until the day his trial was due to start. He never admitted the murder of Rachel until the evidence was so overwhelming that he had no alternative. It is highly unlikely he will ever admit to other offences unless he is shown that the evidence is incontrovertible.

Is there currently evidence against Napper to prove he killed Claire Tiltman? The short answer is 'No.' However, he has never been taken into account as a likely suspect. If he were and the case were to be re-examined with him as the prime suspect, evidence could be forthcoming, as it was in the Nickell enquiry. But he was dismissed by the Kent investigators as being a 'south London boy' and hardly likely to cross the border between London and Kent (It is a common misconception amongst investigators that criminals are somehow subject to police force boundaries). This, despite the fact Napper lived next to Plumstead Railway Station, only four short stops on a direct line to Greenhithe. The Wimbledon investigators took a similar arbitrary view of Napper's inability to travel across London. This insular view of the Kent Police coupled with the misguided information that Napper was in prison during the time of Claire's murder made him a non-starter as a suspect.

Could Napper have done it? This time the short answer is 'Yes.' He had the opportunity as he lived close to where the offence occurred. At the time he was unemployed and living off a redundancy payout. It is well-established that he roamed country lanes and estates, where he walked unnoticed for miles, linking his travels by public transport. If we are looking for a modus operandi, then look no further than Napper. He would follow lone females and then get ahead of them, prior to turning on them, or hiding and attacking them.

The witnesses Lee Hooper and Jacqueline Gower saw a male walking very close behind Claire in London Road just before the attack. The killer must have known the area well to be familiar with the alleyway from London Road to Riverview Road. Another character, bearing a similar description had been seen in the vicinity earlier in the day between 5.15 pm and 5.30 pm (an hour prior to the attack) by witnesses Mr and Mrs Bannister who described a man standing at the corner of London Road and Station Road grinning and smiling to himself. This man they gave a good description of even down to a side parting in his hair.

The witness Kathleen Still saw a male on the non-pavement side of London Road walking down the hill at 6.12 pm (again just before the attack). She described him as white, 5' 9" to 5' 10" aged about 25, wearing a beige jacket and having a 'baby face'. A witness near the scene of the Nickell murder used the same words, 'baby face', to describe the suspect near the scene. Interestingly Kathleen Still further described the man as 'talking to himself', and with a 'happy expression'. The last part is classic Napper behaviour, and her description is a very good likeness of Napper.

The witness Christine Doyle saw a suspect in Riverview Road and very near to the murder scene at the time of the murder walking quickly away from the scene whilst looking back over his shoulder in the direction of the alleyway. She described the man as 'limping' or 'dragging his leg'. Again, the peculiar walk or stooping gait which many witnesses in the Green Chain Walk enquiry commented upon as well as in the Nickell enquiry. Mrs Doyle described the man as 5' 7" to 5' 8" and wearing a light-coloured jacket. Napper did have a peculiar way of walking with a stoop. The mention of leg dragging was interesting and Vincent Wright made enquiries at local hospitals where he discovered Napper had been admitted to the Brook Hospital in January 1993. That hospital was then a large accident and emergency department situated in Shooters Hill. Enquiries at the hospital to discover the reason for Napper's attendance were met with a Data Protection Act wall of silence. His attendance at the hospital may show that he was an in-patient at the time of the murder and exonerate him. They may also show some injury attended to after the murder. Lastly, he may have been discharged from hospital just before Claire's murder after having been treated for mental health issues. Two letters were written by Vincent to Dr Andrew Payne, a consultant forensic psychiatrist at Broadmoor Hospital, asking about Napper's Brook Hospital stay in January 1993. Under confidentiality rules even the dates could not be divulged. Until access is gained to the hospital records it will never be known what Napper was treated for and the details of his visit there.

Christine Doyle's sighting was reinforced a few moments later when three young boys saw a white male near the railway bridge in Station Road. The figure is described as white, male 25 to 28 years with short dark brown hair and wearing a beige, over waist-length, jacket and white training boots. This man appeared to be 'race walking' as he headed off towards Stone Crossing and away from Greenhithe. A direction which caused the CPS to dismiss him as irrelevant as a possible suspect because he wasn't circling back to pick up his Ford Capri, which in the BBC programme was alleged to have been parked at the top of London Road (something never established as a fact).

Of all these witnesses and others, not one picked out Ash-Smith in an identity parade. Additionally, not one was given the same opportunity to pick out Napper. Christine Doyle was revisited by police to see if she could add to the information she had already given. She told the officers she did not know any of the Ash-Smith family and that she may recognise the man she saw near the doctor's surgery again. This information was not put to the test as she was never asked to attend an identity parade. Is it unfair to presume this was because her description of the man she saw walking away from the murder scene bore no resemblance to Colin Ash-Smith?

Napper was so distinctive that, even almost two years after the Green Chain Rapes, witnesses were still able to positively identify him in an identity parade. Compare this to the witness Kathleen Still who had an unobscured good look at the suspect, was within three feet of him and was sure she would recognise him again. In an identity parade she attended three years later, Kathleen failed to identify Ash-Smith.

Studying the property of Napper which was seized after his arrest for the murder of Samantha and Jazmine Bisset it can be established that he purchased, just before the Claire Tiltman murder, a pair of white training boots. He also purchased an expensive knife of the type used in warfare and only available on mail order. These items were never found. As already stressed, the knife Napper purchased was almost identical to the one he bought just before he murdered Rachel Nickell. The knife used in the Nickell attack was also never recovered. These knives were not 'throwaway' items. Even in 1992 they cost over £60 each.

Being careful not to fall into the same trap as the Wimbledon team, care must be taken about getting carried away and making the evidence fit the crime, falling into the dreaded abyss of 'confirmation bias'. However, there is a case for looking at this murder case from a different angle with Napper as a suspect. There are opportunities for further investigation. When a murder review is carried out on a cold case the investigators will avail themselves of all the facts. They will then look for avenues of investigation which were either never pursued or not pursued with appropriate vigour. Once these avenues are identified the reviewer will compile a list of recommendations which will be allocated to an investigating team to carry out.

Having studied the facts in this case I have identified avenues of exploration that I set out under the separate headings below. This would not require a full investigation but isolate a specific list of further enquiries which may or may not identify Napper as the killer of Claire Tiltman.

Shoeprints

There is mention in the available police paperwork of lifts being taken of shoeprints from or near the scene. The reference is in the reports of forensic scientist Heather Carrington dated 26 February 1993 and 30 April 1993. The whereabouts of these 'prints' is unclear and only a full review of the files will produce their current whereabouts. The trainer prints were compared to Ash-Smith's footwear and no match was found. The same prints should be compared to the Adidas Phantom trainer shoeprint found in blood at the scene of the Bisset murders. It is accepted that the actual Adidas trainers were never recovered from Napper, but it can be proved he had purchased an exact same pair prior to the Bisset murders in November 1993. This purchase was by mail order. His Woolwich account shows that the cheque he sent off was cleared on 12 January 1993. It is the case that the trainer shoeprint (known as the composite shoeprint because it was a collection of fragments) was left by Robert Napper. A man was seen by several witnesses leaving the vicinity of the Tiltman crime scene wearing white trainer-type boots.

Robert Napper's clothing

This could be subjected to a DNA examination for traces of Claire Tiltman. This is a basic 'action' to be taken against all possible suspects. As the refinement of DNA comparison continues to improve so do the chances of finding traces of DNA linking suspect to victim. The search would be limited to Napper's outer clothing which bore resemblance to that described by the witnesses. Special attention should be given to the light-coloured jacket as seen in the surveillance photograph taken just prior to arrest in 1994. It is fortunate that during the re-investigation into the Nickell murder a quantity of Napper's clothing from the time of the murder was recovered from storage in Broadmoor Hospital. This clothing should be still preserved within the Metropolitan Police system.

Claire Tiltman's clothing

All Claire's outer clothing should be examined for DNA traces of Napper. This action corresponds to the above. It is accepted that the clothing worn by Claire, in particular her jacket, may have been contaminated when subjected to the various tests given to it at the time, particularly the knife tear comparisons. However, any contamination cannot include cross-contamination from Napper as he has never really entered into the Tiltman enquiry. Remember it took ten years before Napper's DNA was found in the clothing of Rachel Nickell and let us not forget the red flakes of paint found in Alex Hanscombe's (Rachel's son's)[17] hair which matched the toolbox recovered from his bedsit in Plumstead. The importance of the preservation of evidence cannot be stressed enough.

Despite the lack of forensic evidence in the Tiltman case there does remain one DNA question that up until 2014 could not be answered. Unidentified DNA was recovered from the back of Claire's blouse (MJH/15) and the back of her jacket (MJH/8). A report dated 23 October 2014 (one month before the trial of Ash-Smith began), by forensic scientist Susan Woodroffe of Cellmark Forensic Services, describes their

17. Alex took his father's name.

attempts to extract DNA profiles from the samples on these pieces of clothing. A report states:

> 'A full DNA (SGM+1) matching that of Claire Tiltman was obtained from the left shoulder of the blouse. Associated with this profile were additional traces of DNA which could not have originated from Ms Tiltman. The gender marker indicates that there is at least one male contributor to the traces.
>
> Further refinement of this sample was attempted using Y-STR analysis. The Y-STR analysis has not been carried out in duplicate.
>
> The results obtained from this single analysis are weak, incomplete and unconfirmed.
>
> The additional traces of DNA detected in the DNA profile obtained from the blouse (MJH/15) are sufficiently similar to those on the jacket (MJH/8) that the same male could have contributed to all of these results.'

The assailant would have had direct contact with Claire's blouse during the attack. Can this sample be enhanced and further tests carried out on her clothing to be specifically compared with Robert Napper?

Blood distribution

It is absolutely crucial that the blood distribution from the Tiltman murder scene be re-examined by an independent expert. Although the scene is long gone there will be sufficient information for an expert in this subject to make an assessment. As a layman in these matters, I drew the conclusion taking into account the wound patterns and blood distribution on the fence that the assailant would be right-handed. I have attended many murder scenes where the patterns of blood distribution are important to establish what happened and in what order. My own opinion as a non-qualified observer is worthless scientifically speaking, and the scene must be assessed by a scientist to give an opinion which *can* be taken into account. Especially as the prosecutor relied so heavily on the evidence of Dr Heath which (belatedly) gave the opinion the attacker was left-handed, matching their current suspect Ash-Smith. The arterial spray of blood found on the wooden fence at the exit of the alleyway into London Road in all probability came from the final blow inflicted on the victim from behind as she tried to make her escape back towards the London Road. This blow ruptured her aortic artery and as the knife was withdrawn this resulted in a pressurised spray from the knife wound to the fence. She would have been facing down the alley with the fence on her right-hand side. She must have been stabbed from behind at this point. The attacker, to have withdrawn the knife which allowed the blood to escape and to spray the fence, must have held the knife in his right-hand. There is no other way to explain how the blood deposit landed where it did. If the corrected opinion is that the assailant is in all probability right-handed, it would cast serious doubt on the culpability of Ash-Smith. Just as the prosecutor argued that in the opinion of Dr Heath the attacker was left-handed and Ash-Smith is left-handed (which covers only 8% to 10% of the population), an alternative view would turn that assumption on its head and make it highly unlikely to have been Ash-Smith. Incidentally, Robert Napper is right-handed.

Knives and knife wounds

Claire's wounds should be compared with the knives known to have been used by and in the possession of Napper at the time of her murder. Just as the trainers worn by Napper at the Bisset murders were never recovered, neither were those murder weapons. It is known that Napper bought several heavy-duty military-style knives and these were compared to the wounds of Samantha and Rachel and found to be compatible. This is not the best evidence, but rather better than the evidence offered in the Tiltman case where no comparable weapon to fit the crime was ever found in the possession of Ash-Smith. It has been established, however, that Ash-Smith was fascinated by knives and had possessed large ones in his past. The knife he used during his attack on Beverley Godfrey was of the Bowie-style. Although none of his knives could be matched to Claire's wounds, this knife fascination and misuse counted against him.

Napper's interviews

Consideration should be given of further interviews with Napper to give him the opportunity to confess to other attacks (unlikely but attitudes change with age and maturity). Any interview will only be granted if there is some evidence of possible offences for Napper to answer, otherwise the visit would be viewed as a 'fishing expedition'. Other interviews given in his capacity as a patient will be inadmissible as evidence. However, keeping to the ever-optimistic approach there is always the chance he may have a change of heart and reveal the extent of his crimes.

Murder review

There should be an independent review of the Tiltman case with full access to all documents. The allocation of resources to investigate cold case murders are never easy to obtain. In this case, the Kent Police, although approached on numerous occasions by Vincent Wright with his accumulated reports of causes for concern over the conviction of Ash-Smith, have taken the decision that, as they have a conviction for the murder of Claire, they are satisfied justice has been done. It is very difficult for a large organization to alter course once it's path is set. No criticism is intended to be thrown on the team that investigated the Tiltman murder. They, undoubtedly worked hard over many years to land a successful conviction and it is hard to accept, through a combination of circumstances, that they may have been wrong. The only way, even though it may 'stick in their throats', is for the review into the murder to be carried out by another police force. The ideal candidate would be the Metropolitan Police who hold all the relevant records pertaining to Robert Napper.

A polygraph test of Colin Ash-Smith

Such a test which would supplement that of Diane Ash-Smith as to his alibi claim at the time of the murder has been requested on many occasions. All it needs to facilitate it is the agreement of HM Prison Service. It is recognised such a test cannot be used as evidence in English criminal law and procedure. However, if Ash-Smith demonstrates under controlled conditions there is no deceit in his assertion he was with his mother at the time of Claire's death, then, together with her test (*Chapter 20*), it at the very least provides a sound argument for doubt as to his guilt and gives grounds for a murder review.

Method, means and opportunity

There are three things investigators of crime must bear in mind when looking at suspects: *method, means and opportunity*.

Ash-Smith had *method*. He was a proven sexual predator who carried out at least two stranger attacks on lone women. However, the method argument slips when examining the actual attacks on Beverley Godfrey and Charlotte Barnard compared with that on Claire Tiltman. Although his known attacks were vicious and no consideration was given to either victim, and both could have proved fatal, they were not of the frenzied violent nature of the attack on Claire. Claire was known to Ash-Smith whereas his other victims were not.

Ash-Smith had the *means*. He was known to have a fascination with knives and carried in his head fantasies of attacking vulnerable women. Although Ash-Smith did possess and had access to knives of various kinds, only one of them could be shown to be of the type that may have killed Claire (BPO/1). This was a Bowie-type knife that was irrefutably demonstrated to be no longer in his possession at the time of the murder.

Ash-Smith had the *opportunity*. He lived in the area and knew the geography of the streets intimately. But he only had the opportunity if his alibi is a complete sham. There are witnesses to place him elsewhere, there are *no* witnesses to place him near the murder scene.

Robert Napper certainly would pass the *method* test. The savagery of his stranger attacks on women is well-documented and bears close comparison with that on Claire. Also, his known behaviour throughout the period of attacks on the Green Chain Walk are similar, especially towards the end of the series, when they became more violent.

Napper had the means. He was known to be in possession at the time of Claire's murder of more than one hunting knife of the type specifically designed for assault and which would fit the wounds inflicted on Claire Tiltman. I repeat that he had just bought a knife of the type which killed Claire, the same type of weapon he had used in the Bisset and Nickell attacks.

Napper had the opportunity. He was unemployed at the time of the murder and had spare cash from a redundancy payment. Plus, he was residing only a short distance from Greenhithe and was a frequent user of the railway. At this period in his life, it is known he was regularly stalking the footpaths and byways of south east London and Kent and was in the middle of one of the most violent, serial, sexual and murderous attacks on women this country has ever seen.

Robert Napper certainly would pass the *m.o.* test: the severity of his frenzied attacks on women is well-documented and bears close comparison with that on Claire. Also, [illegible] the series of attacks on the Green Chain Walk [illegible] towards the end of the [illegible] when they became more violent.

Napper had the means. He was known to be in possession of the [illegible] on Claire Tiltman [illegible] a knife [illegible] the type which killed Claire [illegible] he had used in the [illegible] attacks.

Napper had the opportunity. He was unemployed at the time of the murder and had spare cash from a redundancy payment. Thus he was residing only a short distance from [illegible] and was a frequent user of the railway. At this period in his life, it is known he was regularly stalking the footpaths and byways of south-east London and Kent and was in the middle of one of the most violent serial rapes and murderous attacks on women this country has ever seen.

Final Thoughts

What else has Robert Napper done? At the time of his evil, progressively more violent crime spree, several other women were attacked and murdered in what may be seen as within the bounds of his modus operandi and his predatory operations. There are potential links to several unsolved murder cases that need exploring. This is not to say that Napper was the *only* psychopathic killer on the loose between 1988 and 1994, but serial killing is, thankfully, a very rare phenomenon. So rare it must focus attention on those whom we know are capable of committing such acts.

Four cases in particular are worthy of further consideration. Those of Debbie Linsley, Jean Bradley, Patricia Parsons and Penny Bell. All these women were attacked when Napper was at his most prolific and all have oblique references in his *A to Zs* and correspondence seized at his flat at the time of his arrest. Vincent Wright has approached the Metropolitan Police concerning all these unsolved cases, always armed with reasoned facts to suggest the offences may have been committed by Napper. Although he has generally been received politely, there has never been any feedback as to whether any of these investigations have considered Napper in their reviews.

There are marks in Napper's *A to Zs* which point to activity in Petts Wood (Debbie Linsley). There are also *A to Z* marks close to where Penny Bell was murdered and in the Kilburn area where she worked. Map markings were also found around the Friern Barnet neighbourhood where Patricia Parsons lived. She was found dead in her car in a rural location, several miles away in Upshire, Epping Forest. It is thought she was murdered by someone using a crossbow. In amongst Napper's many scribblings and doodles the name of a pub was found. A pub not far from where Patricia's body was discovered.

Also worth noting, after the Jean Bradley murder the suspect was chased for some considerable distance from the scene. He was described as having a peculiar loping gait. He was wearing a light-coloured old-fashioned trench coat. Just such a coat was found in Napper's bedsit on his arrest for the murders of the Bissets. Has this coat been submitted for detailed DNA testing against the Jean Bradley crime scene?

It is interesting to record that Napper was known at one time to be in possession of a crossbow. It was found when his address was searched after he had been arrested for trying to have Metropolitan Police headed notepaper printed, together with the first *A to Z* book, the significance of which was not realised at the time. The crossbow was retained by police but not thought of as relevant to the Bisset murders. However, it is thought Patricia Parsons *was* murdered with a crossbow.

These other investigations will require much more work before any concrete links can be made directly to Napper. Speaking from a personal point of view and as someone who has been involved in the investigation of scores of murders, I believe he is a man who was able to operate in the shadows without being seen for the monster he really is.

I believe Robert Clive Napper could yet be found to be one of the most prolific serial killers ever to stalk the streets, woods and lanes of this country. Never being seen as he wrapped himself in his cloak of ordinariness: 'Now you see me, now you don't.'

Index

Also by Alan Jackaman

Napper
Through a Glass Darkly

Napper records the tragic circumstances which led to one man committing a sequence of attacks known as The Green Chain Rapes through to the murders of Rachel Nickell and Samantha and Jazmine Bisset. It took Alan Jackaman 25 years to come to terms with what he experienced, but in this his acclaimed earlier work he tells of his part in the downfall of serial killer Robert Napper.

Paperback, hardback and ebook | ISBN 978-1-909976-70-2

www.ingramcontent.com/pod-product-compliance
Lightning Source LLC
Chambersburg PA
CBHW010734270326
41935CB00016B/1800

* 9 7 8 1 9 1 4 6 0 3 3 6 5 *